Instant Art for Advent and Christmas

Compiled and illustrated
by
Kathryn Atkins

First published in 1995 in Great Britain by
KEVIN MAYHEW LTD
Rattlesden
Bury St Edmunds, Suffolk IP30 0SZ

Catalogue No 1396037
ISBN 0 86209 687 1

© 1995 Kevin Mayhew Ltd
The contents of this book can be photocopied
without copyright infringement, provided they
are intended for non-commercial use

Cover by Sara Silcock
Typesetting by Vicky Brown
Printed in Great Britain

Introduction

Bring the Christmas story alive with this wide variety of Advent and Christmas activities, including a crib, cards, decorations, puzzles and exciting action models. This collection has something for a wide variety of ages, and is ideal for use in many situations: day schools, mid-week clubs, family services, Sunday schools, nurseries, playgroups or at home.

• **suggestions for use**

For some of the activities you may want to tell the story in some way, e.g. drama, storytelling, puppets, overhead projector drawing. Other activities could be used for more extended craft sessions through Advent – for example, the frieze which consists of five colouring pictures, plus a page with a storyline to be glued under each picture.

You will need to photocopy one for each child – unless you are working together on a group project, for example, assembling the crib model. Most of the activities would be better on card but some only need paper. Always encourage the children to colour in parts of any model *before* assembling it.

• **photocopying onto card**

Most photocopiers will take a fine grade of card, and photocopying models straight onto card rather than gluing a paper copy to card achieves a much better and quicker result.

Fine card (A4 size) suitable for photocopying should be available in large packs from suppliers of photocopy paper or from printers. The card will probably need to be *hand fed* into the photocopier, but this does not take too long.

• **equipment required**

It is a good idea to make up make up one model yourself at home at first – this gives you a knowledge of the steps to follow and the equipment you will need, and gives the children a visual demonstration of the finished model.

Good Scissors An essential, but should have round points.

Colouring Pens Cheap packs of felt tip pens are readily available.

Crayons Better for young children for some of the activities.

Glue Solid stick glue with a twist-up end is best. It is quite expensive, but holds in place well for small tabs etc and is not too messy.

Paper Fasteners Available from stationers in boxes of 100 (size 15mm is a useful size).

Sharp point A compass is useful to pierce holes before inserting paper fasteners. *NB piercing holes only to be done by an adult for safety.*

Stapler Invest in a heavy duty stapler.

Craft knife Only to be used by an adult for safety – This is useful in some models for cutting slits or small windows. This should be done before the children's craft session. Just make the appropriate slits/cuts in all the A4 sheets before pieces are cut out. Rest on a piece of hardboard.

Foldlines are marked as follows and will be easier to fold if they are very lightly scored before folding.
– – – – – fold outwards (or 'mountain fold')
– · – · – · fold inwards (or 'valley fold')

Tinsel and Glitter Use your initiative to decorate the crib, cards, mobile, decorations, etc with tinsel or glitter – it really does add a bit of excitement for the children! Glitter glue is less messy than loose glitter.

Contents

1. Crib scene – Mary, Joseph and Shepherd
2. Crib scene – Three Wise Men
3. Crib scene – Baby Jesus, Manger, Gold and Frankincense
4. Crib scene – Animals and Star
5. Crib scene – Stable base
6. Crib scene – Stable roof
7. Crib scene – Stable left side
8. Crib scene – Stable right side
9. Crib scene – Stable pillars
10. Stand-up nativity card
11. Angels and Shepherds card pop-out
12. Stand-up Angel Christmas card
13. Christmas tree model
14. Light of the World Christmas lantern
15. Christmas Angel model
16. Christmas Crown – names of Jesus
17. Christmas Plate decoration
18. Walking Shepherd
19. Angels and Shepherds – Action model
20. Christmas frieze – Gabriel tells Mary about Jesus' birth
21. Christmas frieze – Mary and Joseph go to Bethlehem
22. Christmas frieze – Jesus is born in the Stable
23. Christmas frieze – Angels appear to the Shepherds
24. Christmas frieze – Wise Men follow the Star
25. Christmas frieze – Storylines for pictures 20-24
26. Prophecies about Jesus' birth – Spinner part one
27. Prophecies about Jesus' birth – Spinner part two
28. An Angel tells Zechariah about the birth of John – Action model
29. No Room at the Inn – Action model
30. Angels and Dreams in the Christmas story – Spinner
31. Pop-up Stable Christmas card – Figures and roof
32. Pop-up Stable Christmas card – Base
33. Wise Men follow the Star – Action model
34. Simeon and Anna – Action model
35. A. Expanding Angel decoration.   B. Dove of Peace tree decoration
36. A. Expanding Angel – Body.   B. Dove of Peace – Wings
37. Christmas mobile – Stable roof
38. Christmas mobile – Star, Baby Jesus, Animals
39. Christmas mobile – Mary, Joseph, King, Shepherd
40. Sheep face Baseball Cap
41. Christmas window picture
42. Christmas crossword
43. Christmas puzzle page
44. Advent calendar – Part one
45. Advent calendar – Part two
46. Flight into Egypt – Action model

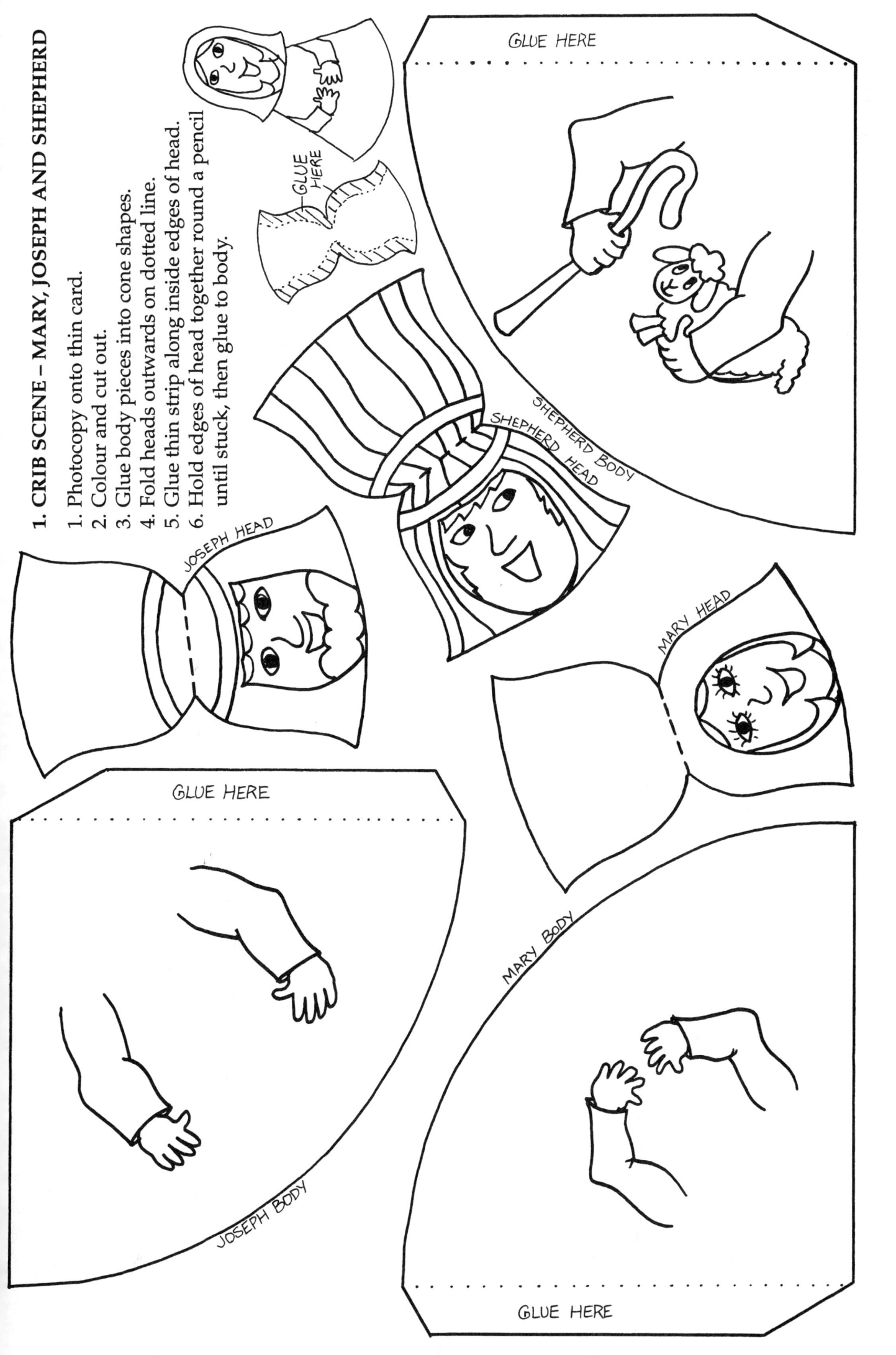

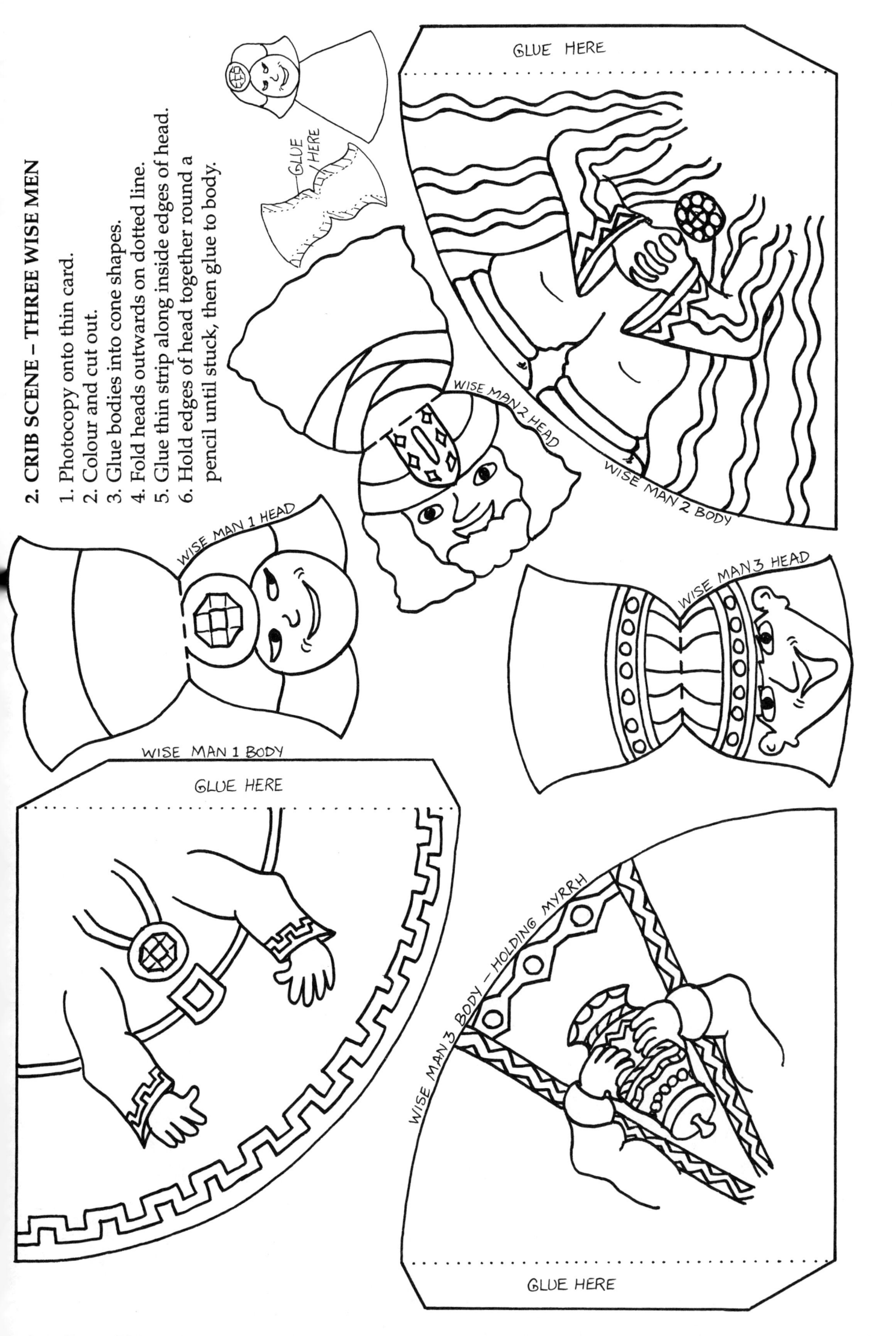

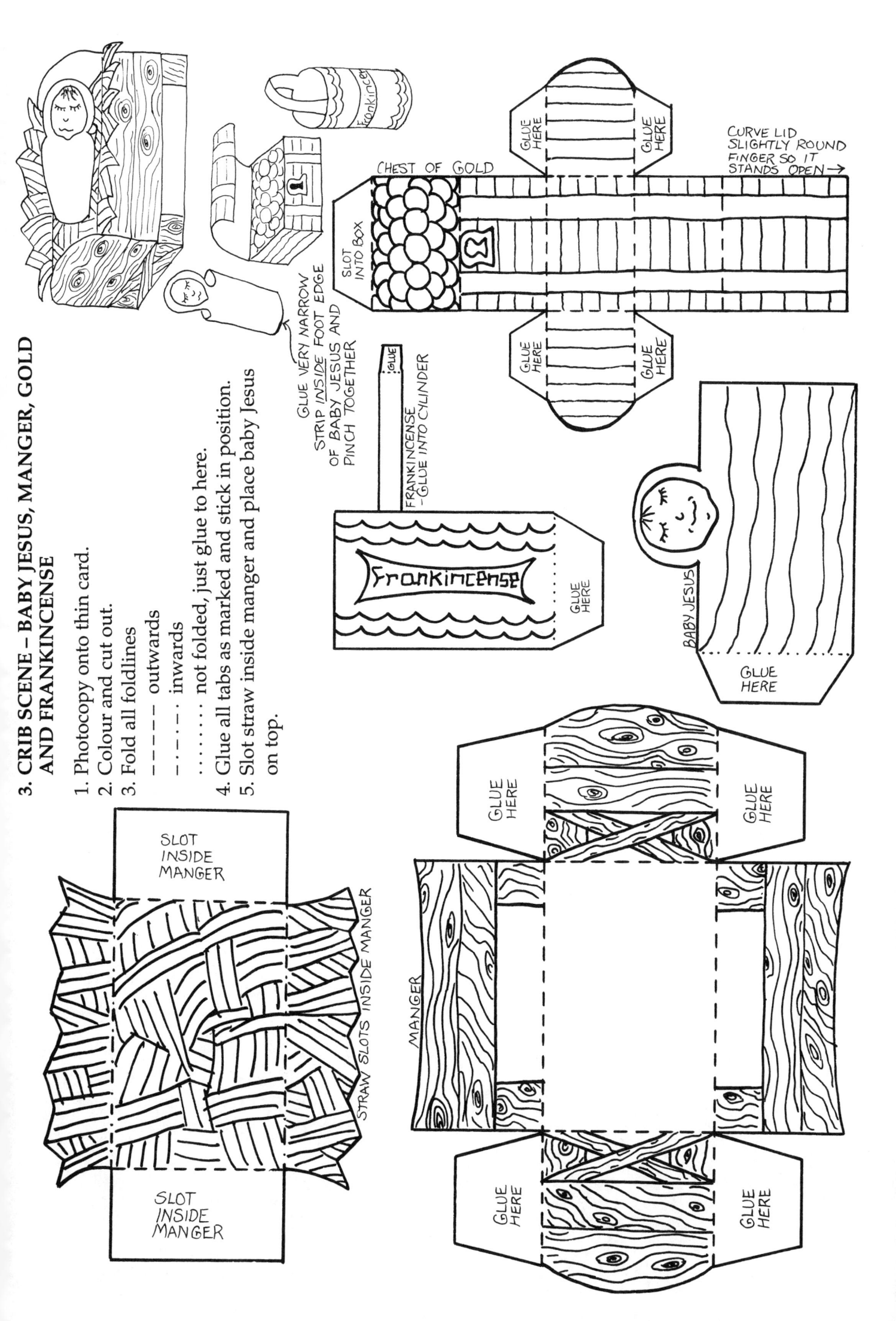

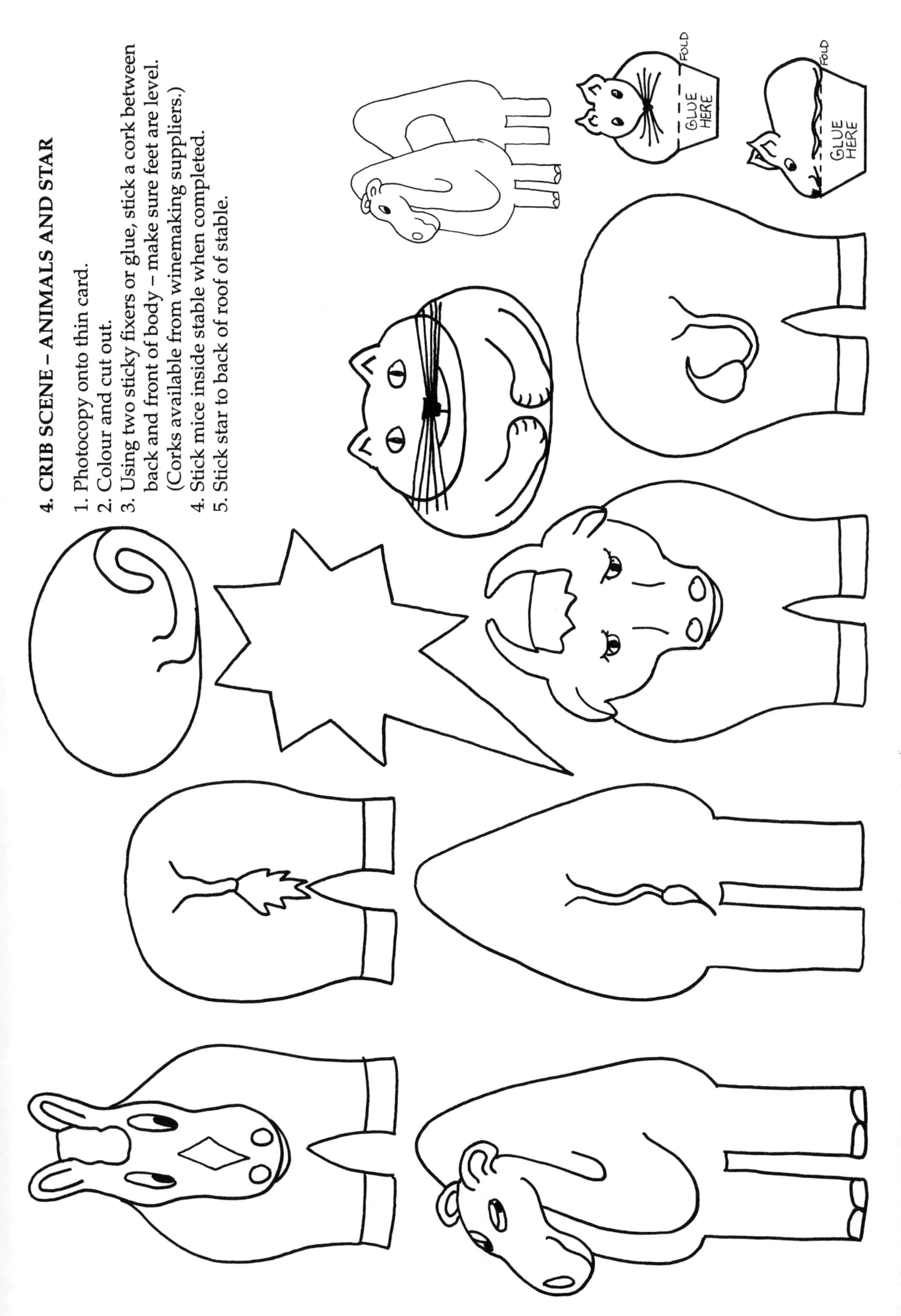

5. CRIB SCENE – STABLE BASE

1. Photocopy onto card and cut out. 2. Cut all slots as marked (by adult using craft knife).

P . . . . GLUE STABLE ROOF TAB HERE . . . . Q

H
I

W
X

J
K

- - - FOLD IN -

L
M

Y
Z

N
O

A
B

C
D

GLUE PILLAR HERE

GLUE PILLAR HERE

6. CRIB SCENE – STABLE ROOF 1. Photocopy onto thin card. 2. Colour and cut out. 3. Fold out on all dotted - - - - foldlines. 4. Glue two small tabs under front edges of roof eaves. 5. Glue long back tab PQ to top back of stable wall.

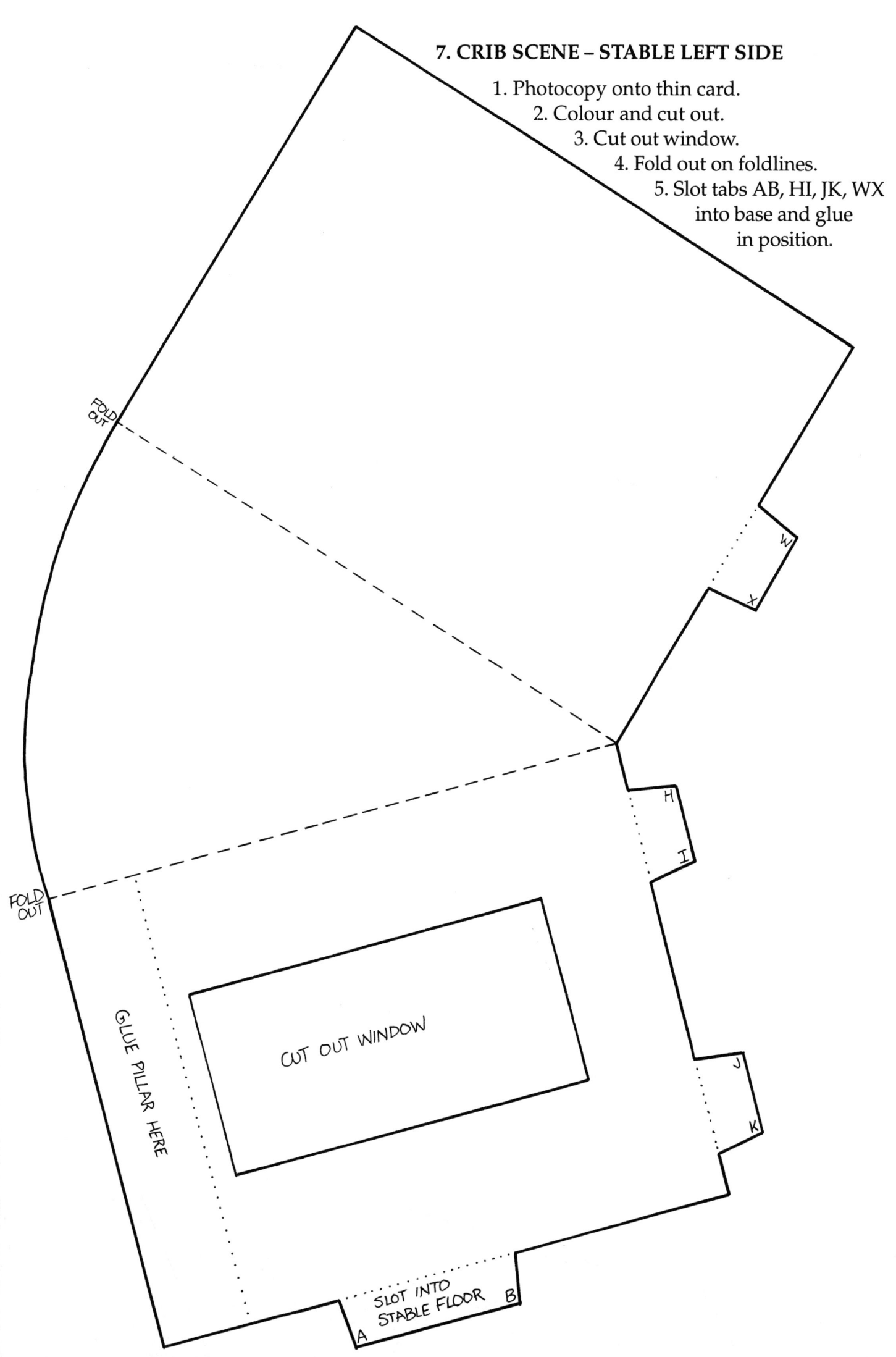

8. CRIB SCENE – STABLE RIGHT SIDE

1. Photocopy onto thin card.
2. Colour and cut out.
3. Cut out window.
4. Fold out on foldlines.
5. Slot tabs CD, LM, NO, YZ into slots on stable base and glue in position.

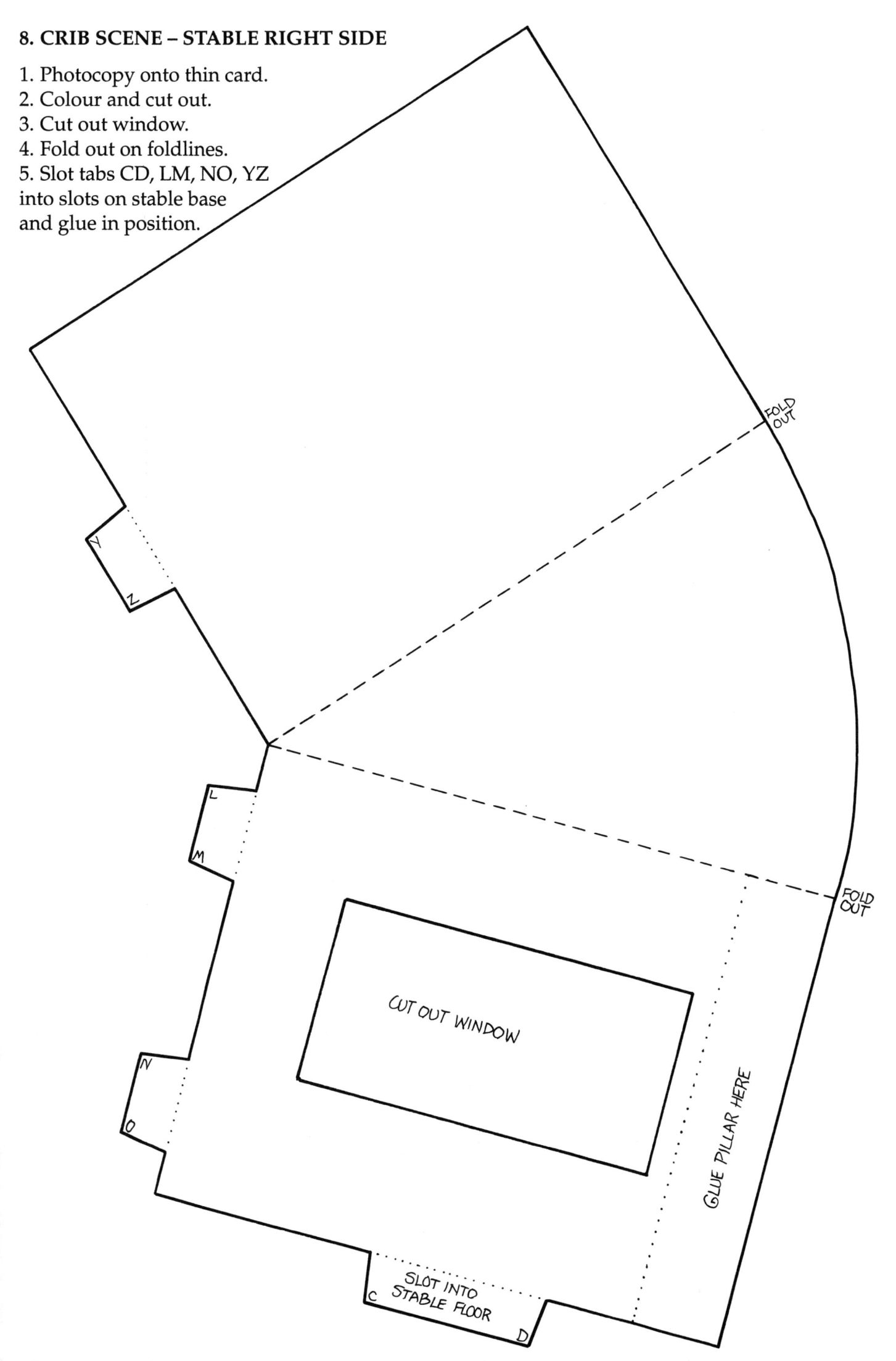

9. CRIB SCENE – STABLE PILLARS

1. Photocopy onto thin card.
2. Colour and cut out.
3. Fold out on all foldlines -----
4. Glue one long side and base of each pillar and glue in position on stable base and against side wall.

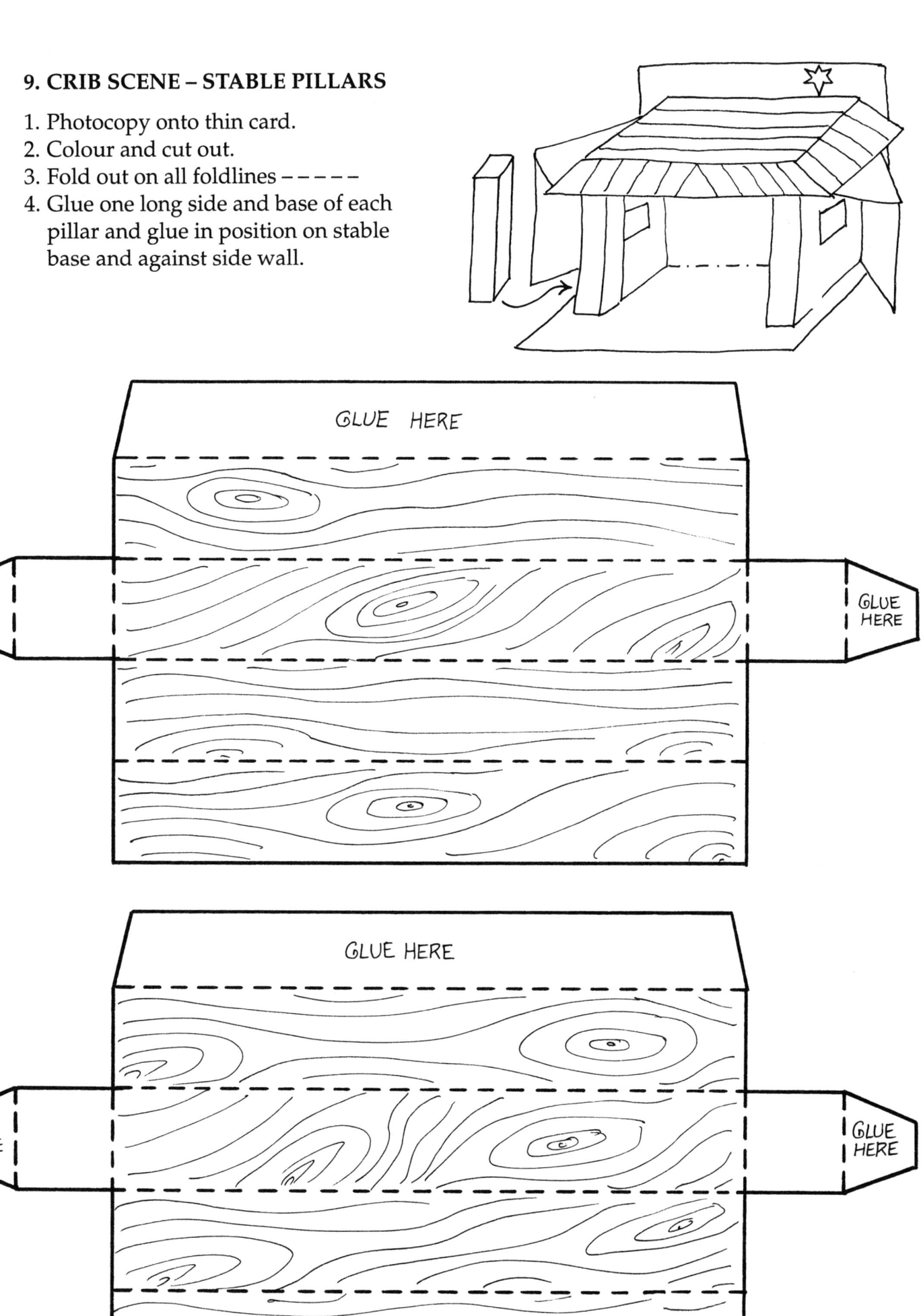

10. STAND-UP NATIVITY CARD

1. Photocopy onto thin card.
2. Colour and cut out.
3. Cut out top three points of star **only** on thick line so it stands out (an adult using a craft knife will give the best result).
4. Fold rest of card out along foldline - - - - -

Happy Christmas

with love from

11. ANGELS AND SHEPHERDS CARD POP-OUT

1. Photocopy onto thin card.
2. Colour and cut out.
3. Score gently along foldlines.
4. Fold carefully along foldlines
   – – – – outwards
   – · – · – inwards.
5. Angel will pop-up when you open card.
6. Draw your own design on outside of card.

An angel of the Lord appeared to them and the glory of the Lord shone around them and they were terrified.

But the angel said to them, "Do not be afraid. I bring you good news of great joy that will be for all the people."

ANGEL POPS UP FROM CARD

FOLD IN
FOLD OUT
FOLD IN
CUT ROUND OUTLINE

12. STAND-UP ANGEL CHRISTMAS CARD

1. Photocopy onto thin card.
2. Colour and cut out.
3. Cut round shoulders and head of angel on thick black line so it will stand out. (Best done by an adult using a craft knife.)
4. Fold rest of card along foldline.

Happy Christmas

with love from

A Saviour has been born to you; he is Christ the Lord

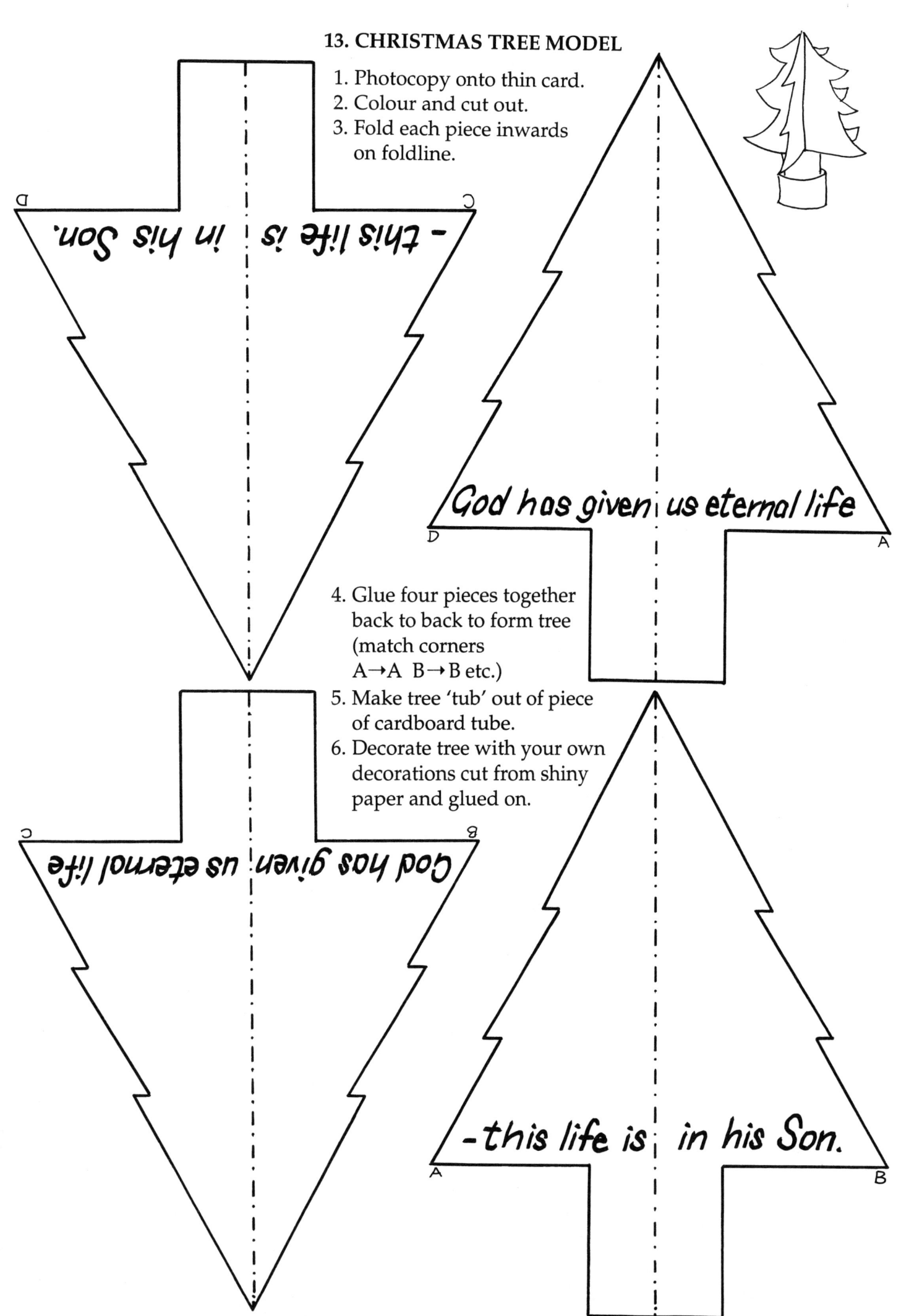

14. LIGHT OF THE WORLD CHRISTMAS LANTERN

1. Photocopy onto paper.
2. Decorate lantern and cut out.
3. Cut off strip at end for handle.
4. Fold lantern in half along foldline – – – –.
5. Cut all parallel slits marked by solid line – cut through **both** thicknesses of paper.
6. Open lantern out and glue into cylinder.
7. Glue handle onto top.

Jesus said: I am the Light of the World

Whoever follows me will never walk in darkness, but will have the light of life. *John 3 v 12*

15. CHRISTMAS ANGEL MODEL

1. Photocopy onto paper.
2. Cut out circle.
3. Draw pattern on wings front and back. Colour in angel.
4. Cut down centre back thick black line and around head but taking care **not** to cut through neck.
5. Fold in on foldlines –·–·–·– and staple dotted foldlines together so angel body forms a cone shape.

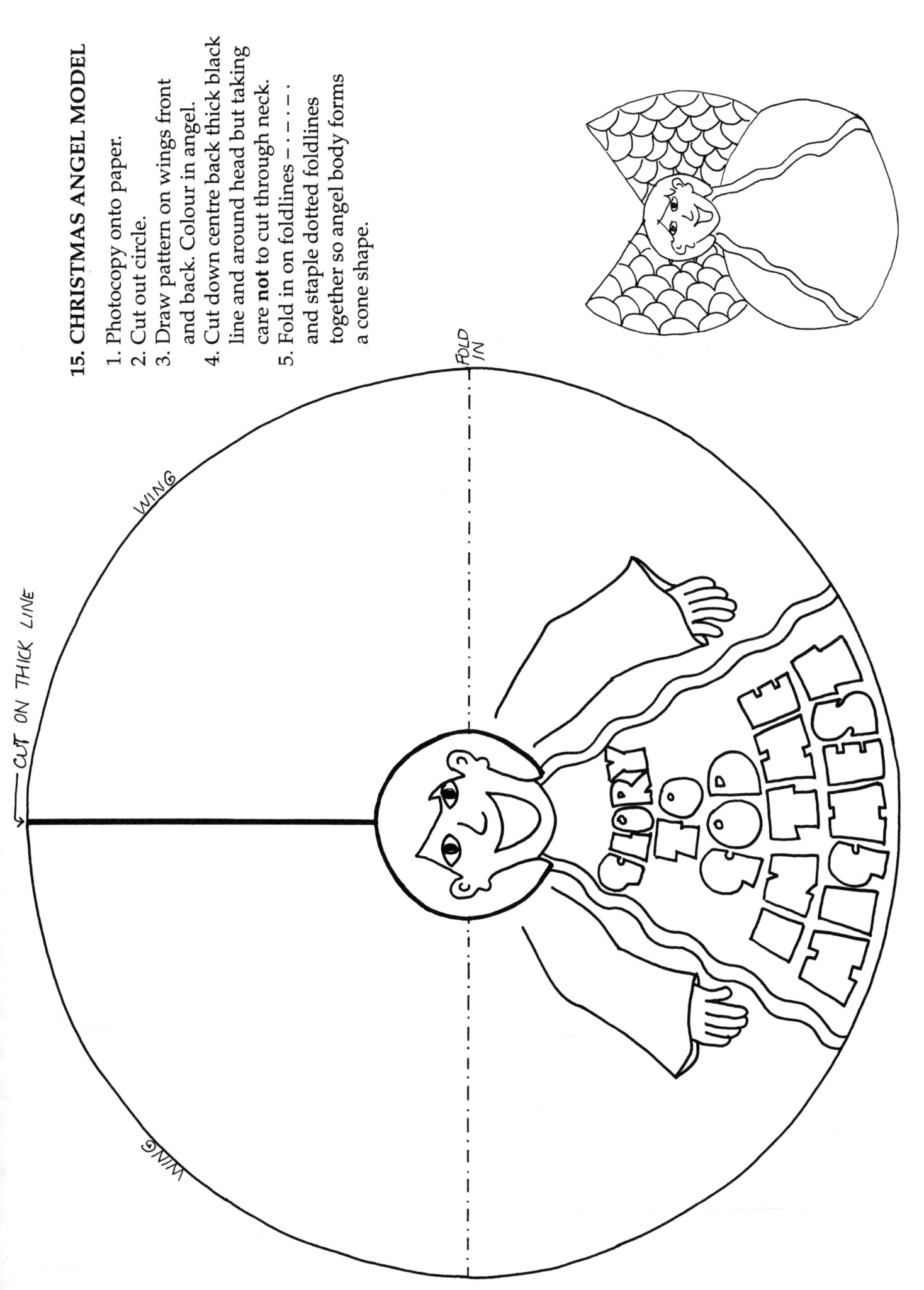

17. CHRISTMAS PLATE DECORATION

1. Photocopy onto thin card.
2. Colour and cut out.
3. Decorate the rim of a large paper plate with your own pattern.
4. Stick the pieces onto the plate using sticky fixers (better than glue, as they give a slight stand-out effect).
5. Staple some tinsel to the top of the plate.

King of Kings

18. WALKING SHEPHERD

1. Photocopy onto thin card.
2. Colour and cut out.
3. Glue 'foot' circles together back to back.
4. Pierce dots A, B, C, D – put paper fastener through A, B, C, D.
5. Staple top of head together.

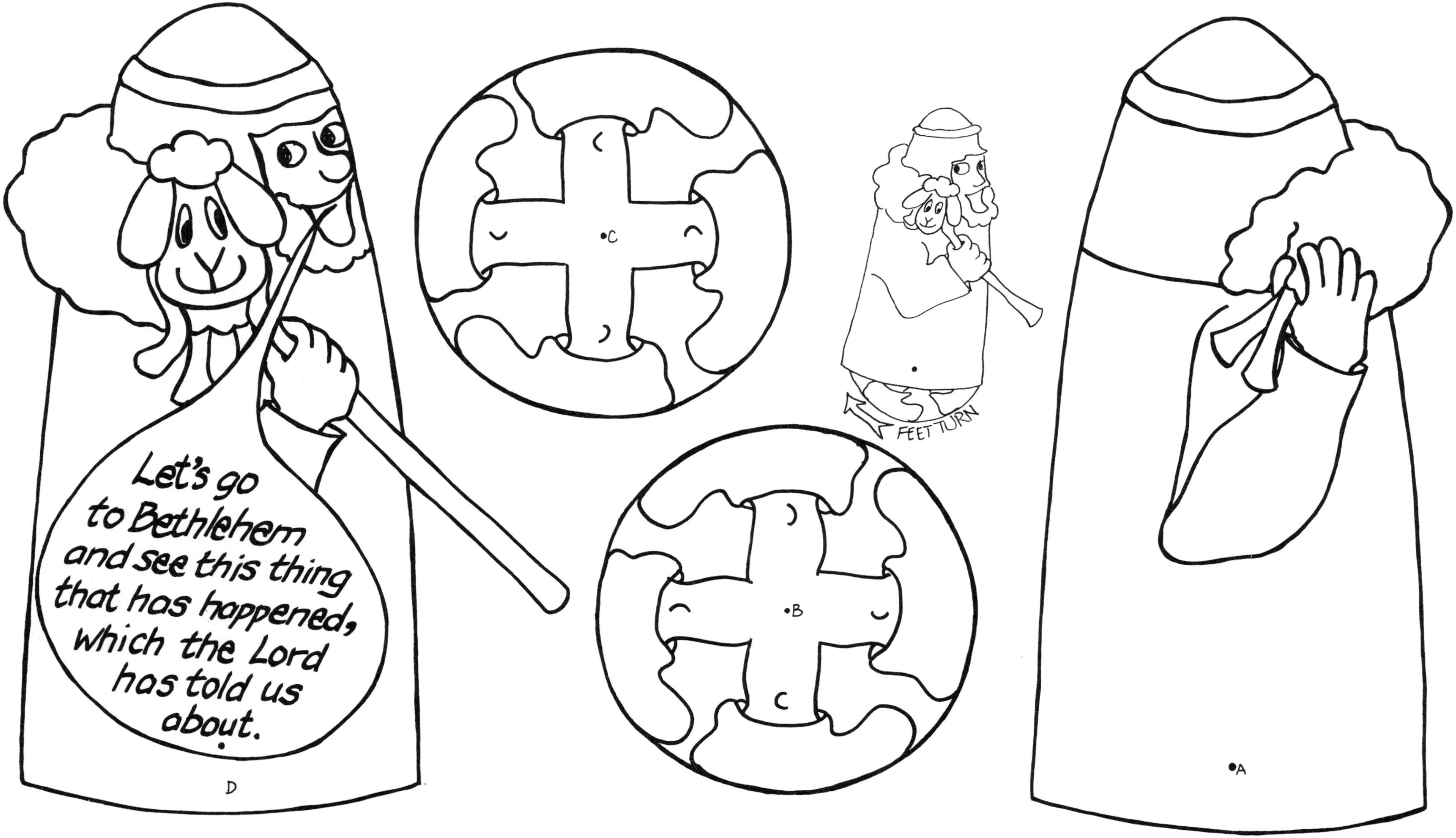

Let's go to Bethlehem and see this thing that has happened, which the Lord has told us about.

19. ANGELS AND SHEPHERDS – ACTION MODEL

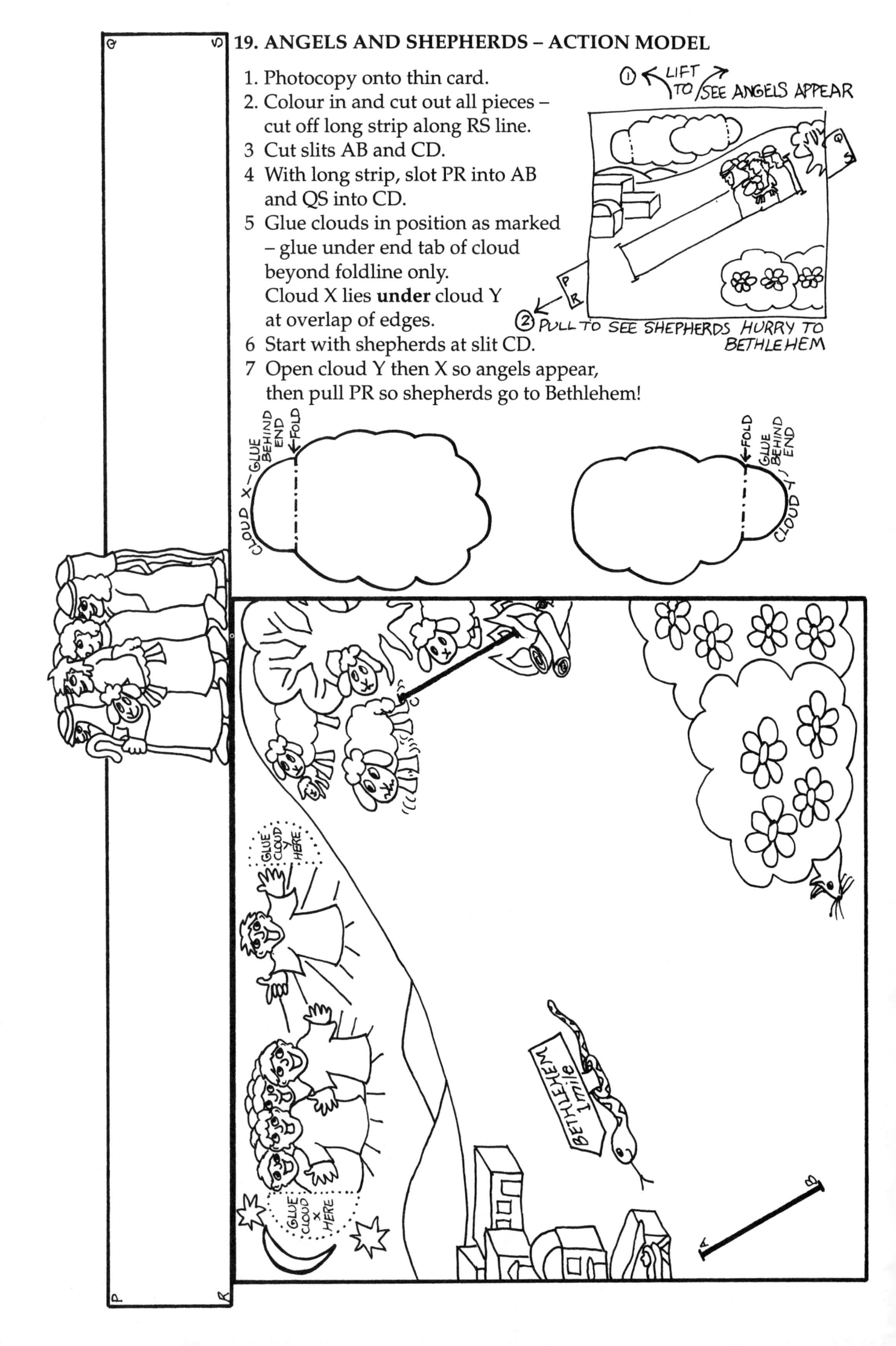

1. Photocopy onto thin card.
2. Colour in and cut out all pieces – cut off long strip along RS line.
3. Cut slits AB and CD.
4. With long strip, slot PR into AB and QS into CD.
5. Glue clouds in position as marked – glue under end tab of cloud beyond foldline only.
   Cloud X lies **under** cloud Y at overlap of edges.
6. Start with shepherds at slit CD.
7. Open cloud Y then X so angels appear, then pull PR so shepherds go to Bethlehem!

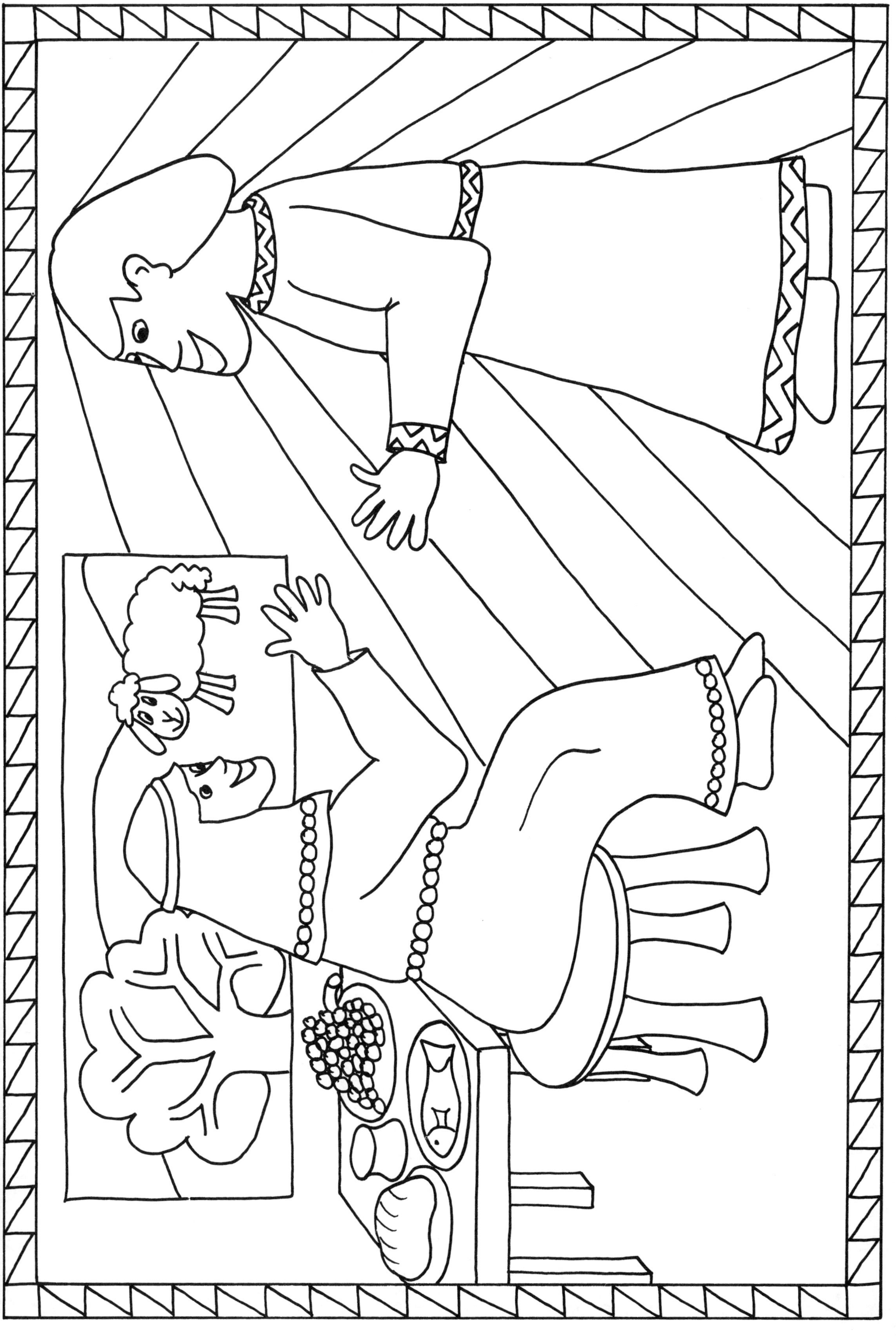

Bethlehem

Full Roman Breakfast Included in Price
NO VACANCIES
Sorry, Full Up
THE STAR INN
30 ROOMS All horsehair mattresses
B+B
NO ROOMS LEFT
STABLE This Way

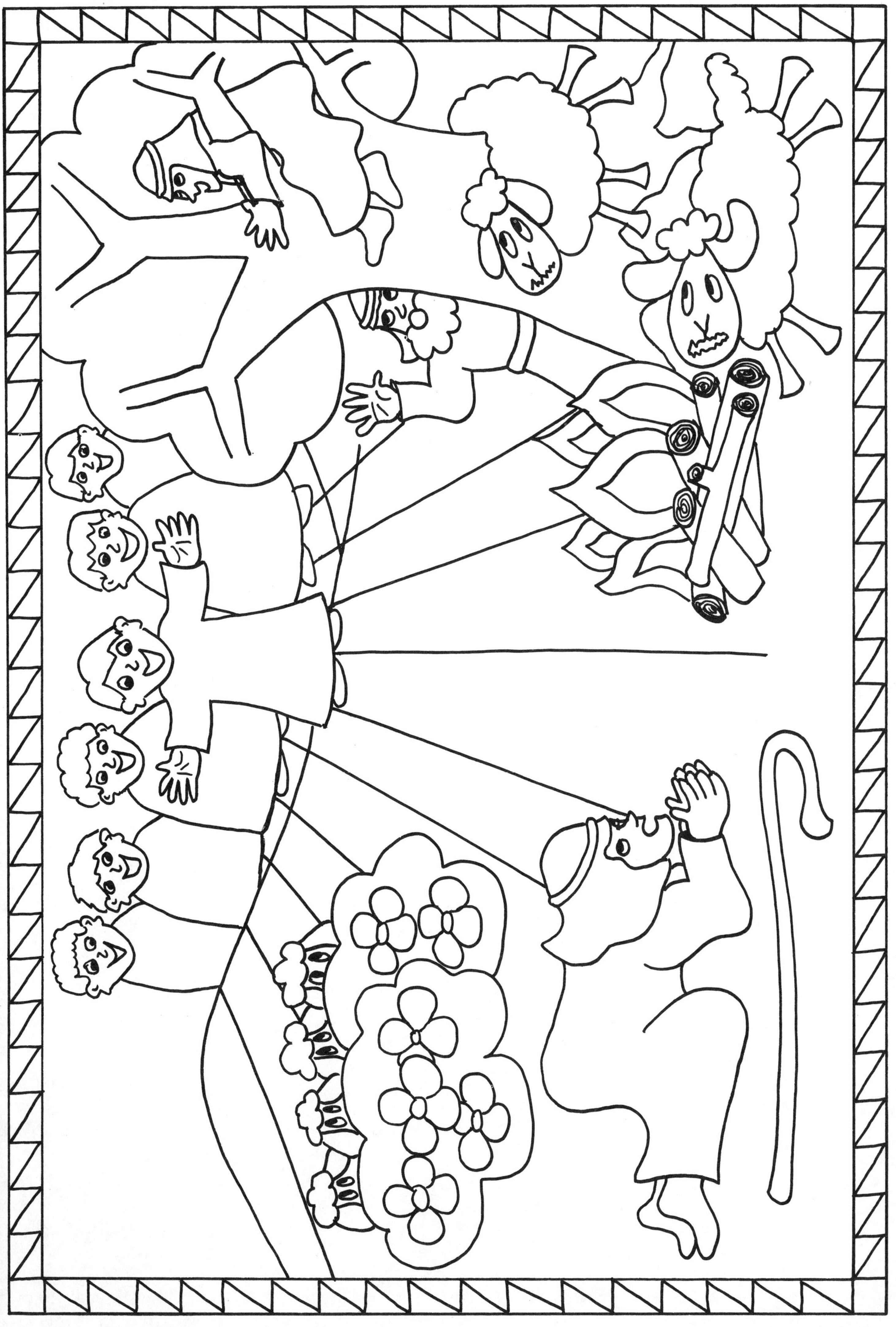

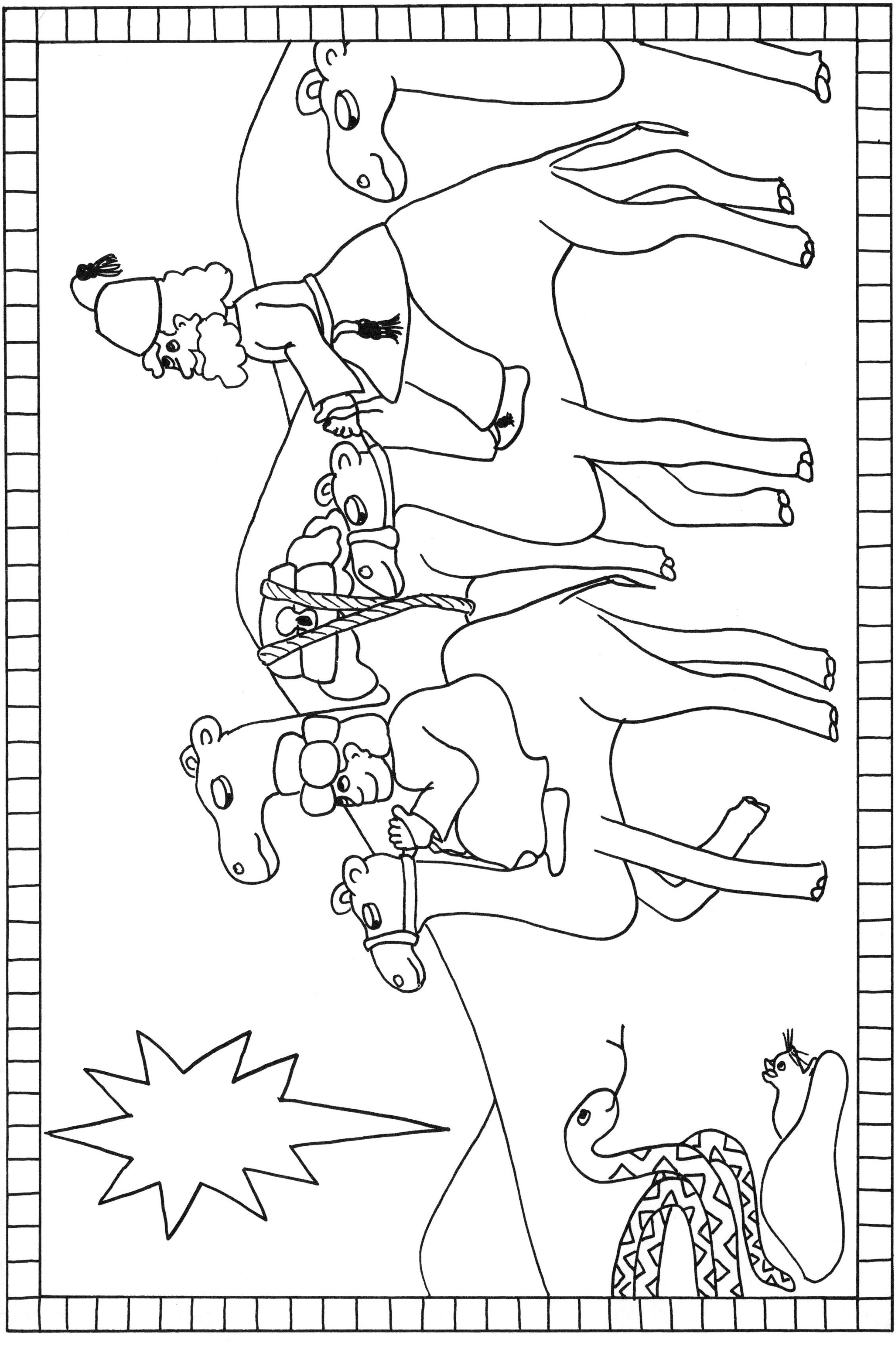

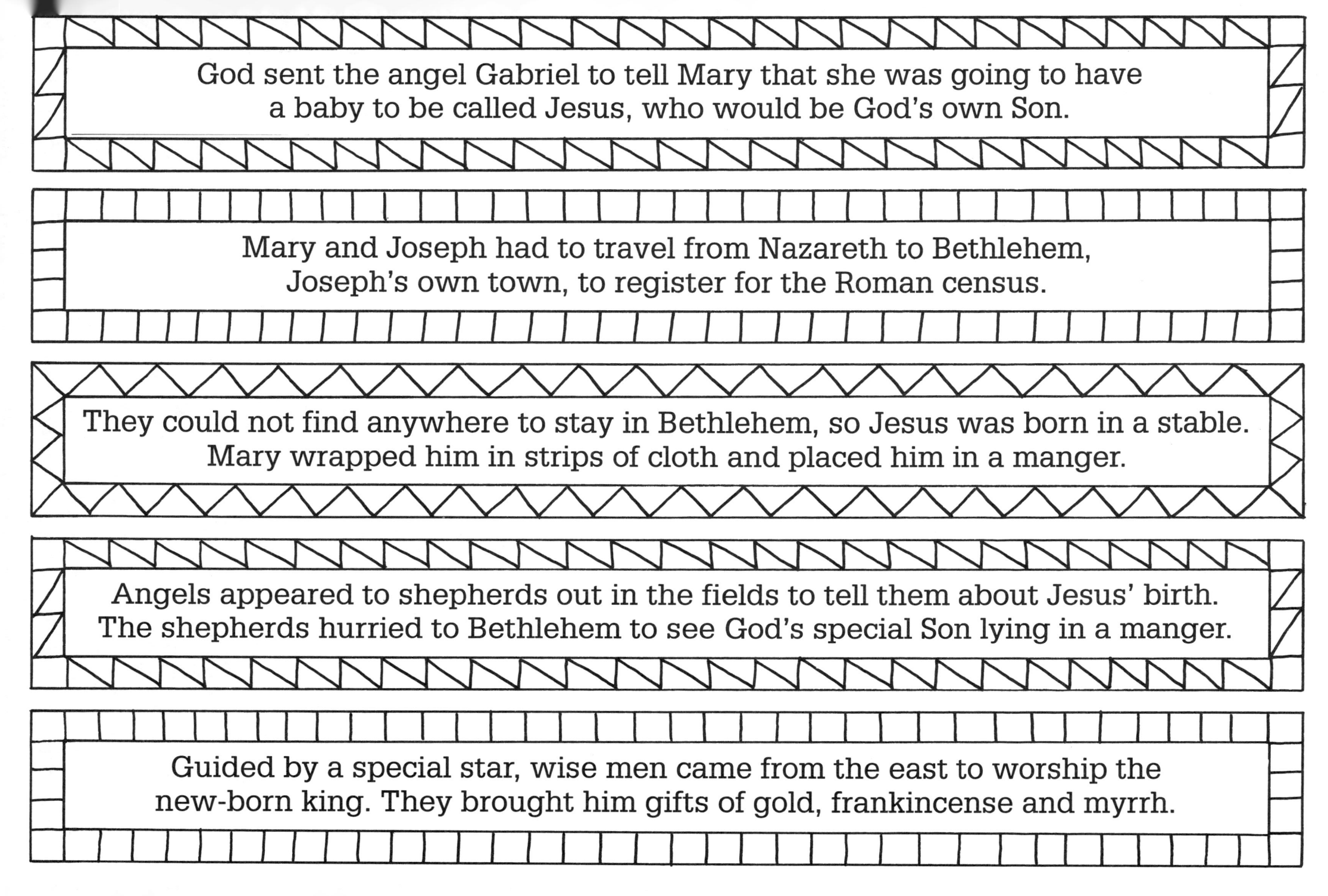

God sent the angel Gabriel to tell Mary that she was going to have a baby to be called Jesus, who would be God's own Son.

Mary and Joseph had to travel from Nazareth to Bethlehem, Joseph's own town, to register for the Roman census.

They could not find anywhere to stay in Bethlehem, so Jesus was born in a stable. Mary wrapped him in strips of cloth and placed him in a manger.

Angels appeared to shepherds out in the fields to tell them about Jesus' birth. The shepherds hurried to Bethlehem to see God's special Son lying in a manger.

Guided by a special star, wise men came from the east to worship the new-born king. They brought him gifts of gold, frankincense and myrrh.

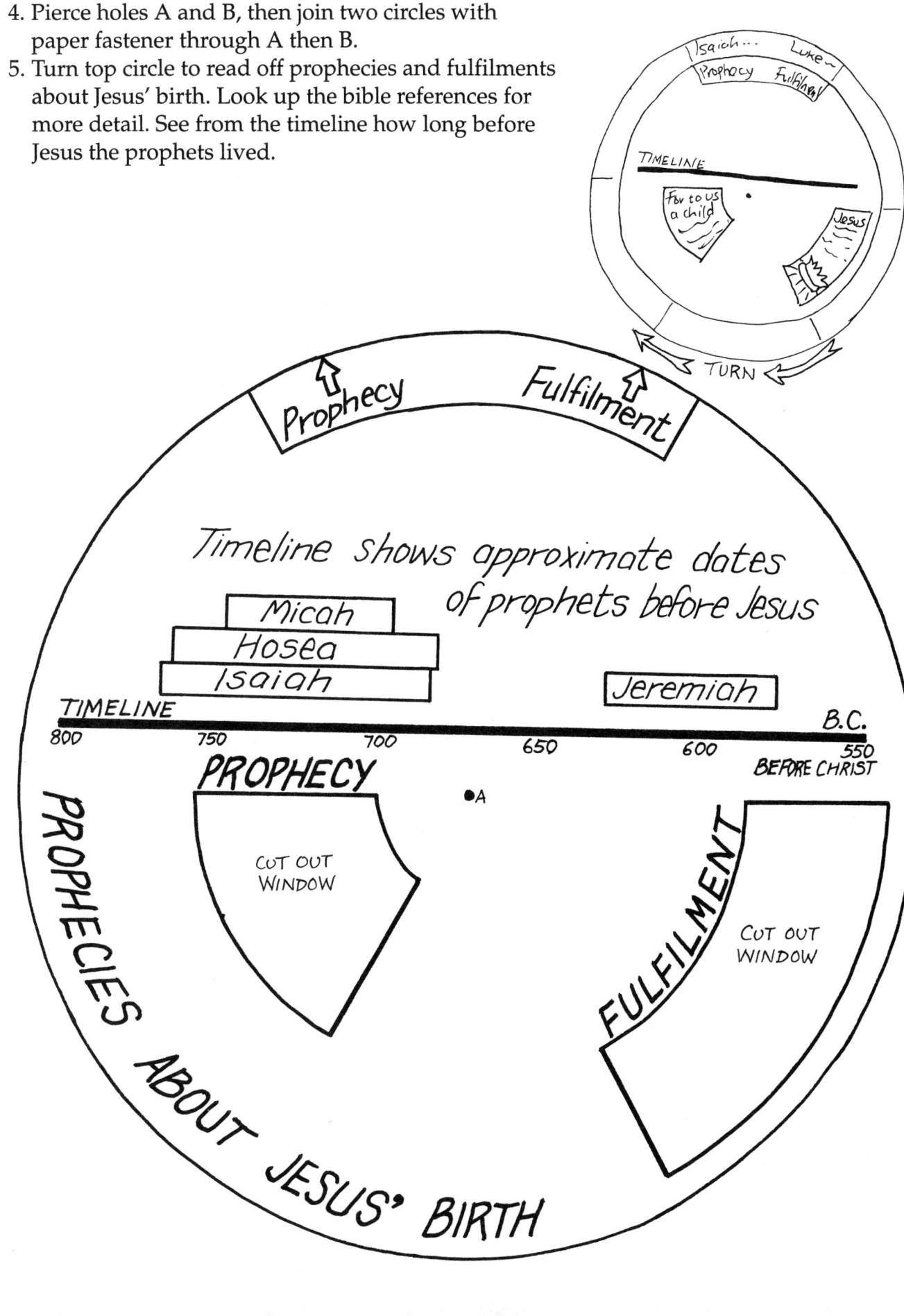

26. PROPHECIES ABOUT JESUS' BIRTH – SPINNER PART ONE

1. Photocopy this and following page onto thin card.
2. Colour and cut out.
3. Cut out two windows in top circle (this page).
4. Pierce holes A and B, then join two circles with paper fastener through A then B.
5. Turn top circle to read off prophecies and fulfilments about Jesus' birth. Look up the bible references for more detail. See from the timeline how long before Jesus the prophets lived.

Prophecy | Fulfilment

Timeline shows approximate dates of prophets before Jesus

- Micah
- Hosea
- Isaiah
- Jeremiah

TIMELINE
800 — 750 — 700 — 650 — 600 — 550
B.C. BEFORE CHRIST

PROPHECY — CUT OUT WINDOW
• A
FULFILMENT — CUT OUT WINDOW

PROPHECIES ABOUT JESUS' BIRTH

27. PROPHECIES ABOUT JESUS' BIRTH – SPINNER PART TWO

See previous page for instructions.

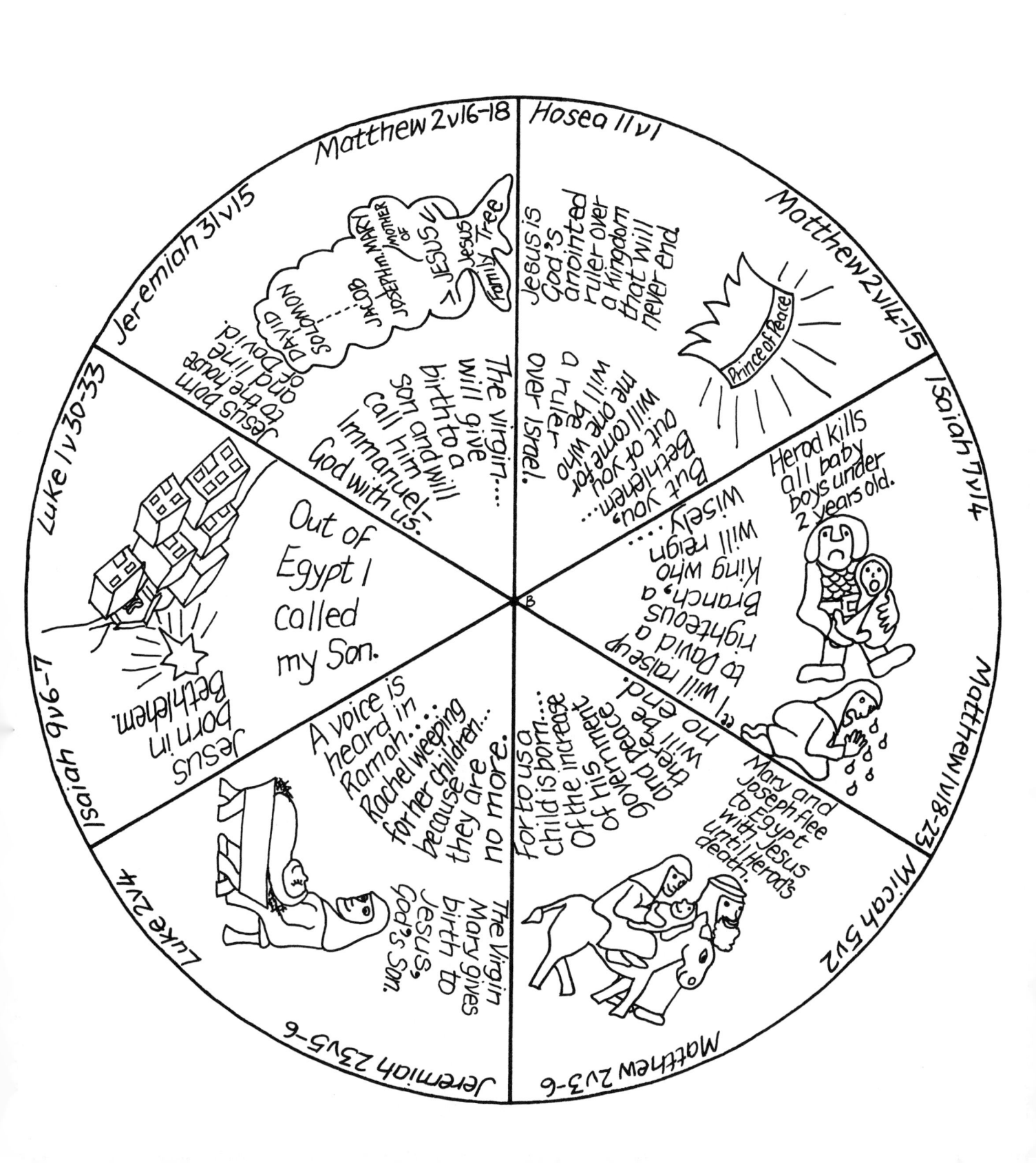

28. AN ANGEL TELLS ZECHARIAH ABOUT THE BIRTH OF JOHN – ACTION MODEL

1. Photocopy onto thin card.
2. Colour and cut out all three pieces.
3. Fold main piece on all foldlines
   - – – – – – outwards
   - – . – . – . inwards.
4. Cut slit XY.
5. Glue marked dotted rectangles on backing piece.
6. Line up pillar CD over left edge of backing piece, and corners E and F over small glued rectangles. Press onto glue.
7. Pierce dots A, B. Slot arm through slit XY and slot paper fastener through A, B.

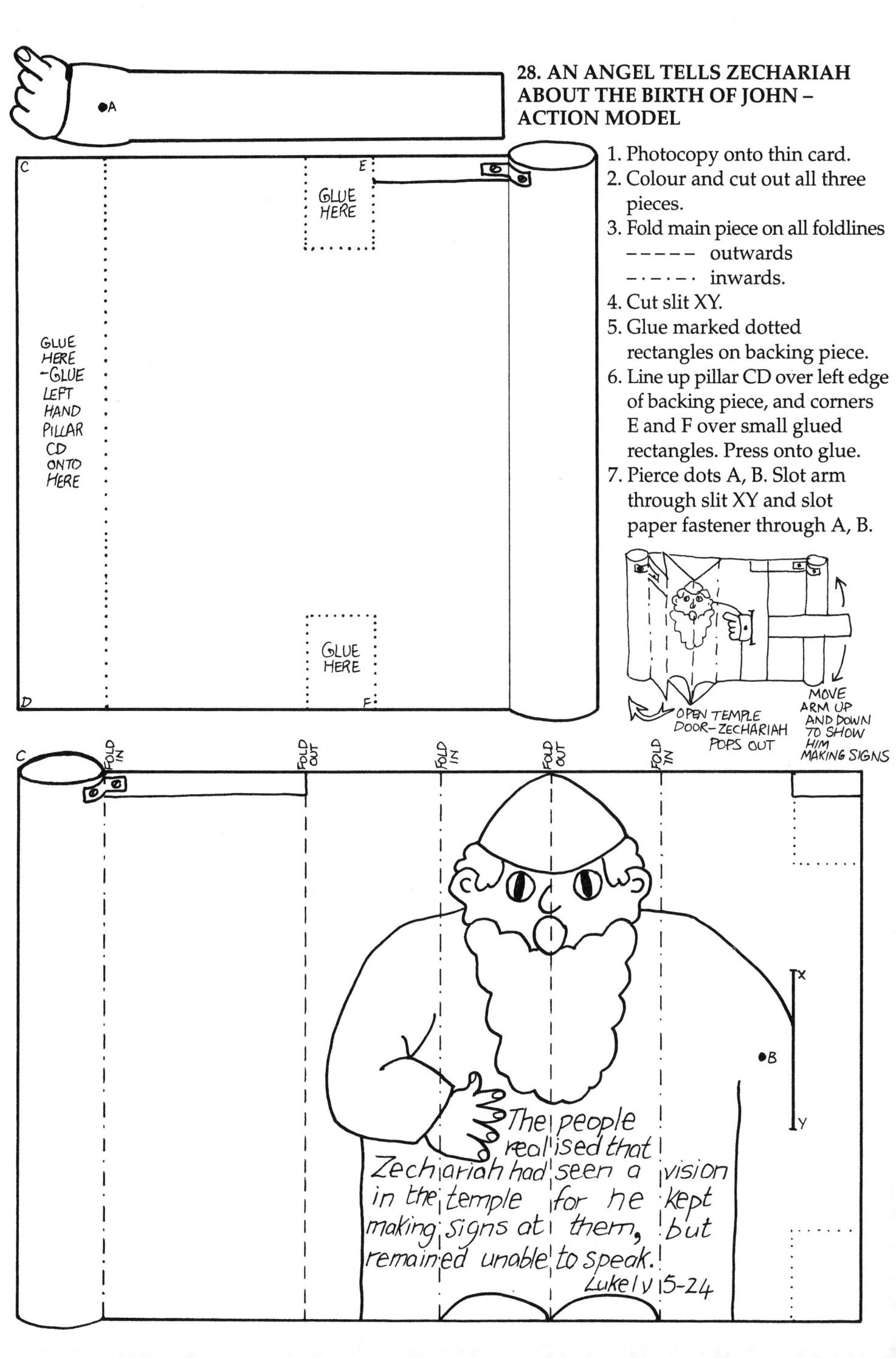

OPEN TEMPLE DOOR – ZECHARIAH POPS OUT

MOVE ARM UP AND DOWN TO SHOW HIM MAKING SIGNS

The people realised that Zechariah had seen a vision in the temple for he kept making signs at them, but remained unable to speak.

Luke I v 15-24

29. NO ROOM AT THE INN – ACTION MODEL

1. Photocopy onto thin card.
2. Colour and cut out.
3. Cut slits AB and CD.
4. Cut thick black slits round three sides of inn door only and fold along dotted line – · – · – · so that door opens.
5. Fold inwards on dotted line – · · – · · – on long strip.
6. Slot end XY of long strip up through slit CD, down through AB, and up through open door.
7. Glue **behind** folded end XY then glue to inside of door edge XY.

PULL TO CLOSE DOOR AGAIN – OPEN DOOR TO SEE INNKEEPER COME OUT AND MARY AND JOSEPH COME ALONG STREET.

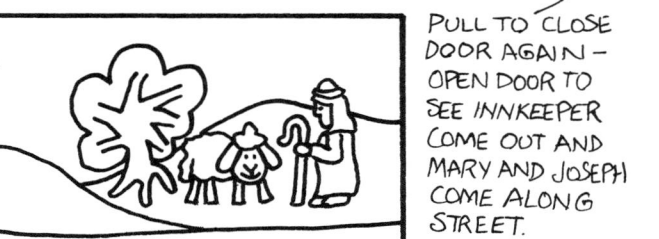

OPEN DOOR

GLUE XY TO INSIDE EDGE

30. ANGELS AND DREAMS IN THE CHRISTMAS STORY – SPINNER

1. Photocopy onto thin card.
2. Colour and cut out.
3. Cut out two windows in top circle.
4. Pierce dots A and B.
5. Join two circles with paper fastener through A then B.
6. Turn top circle to read where angels and dreams occur in the Christmas Story.

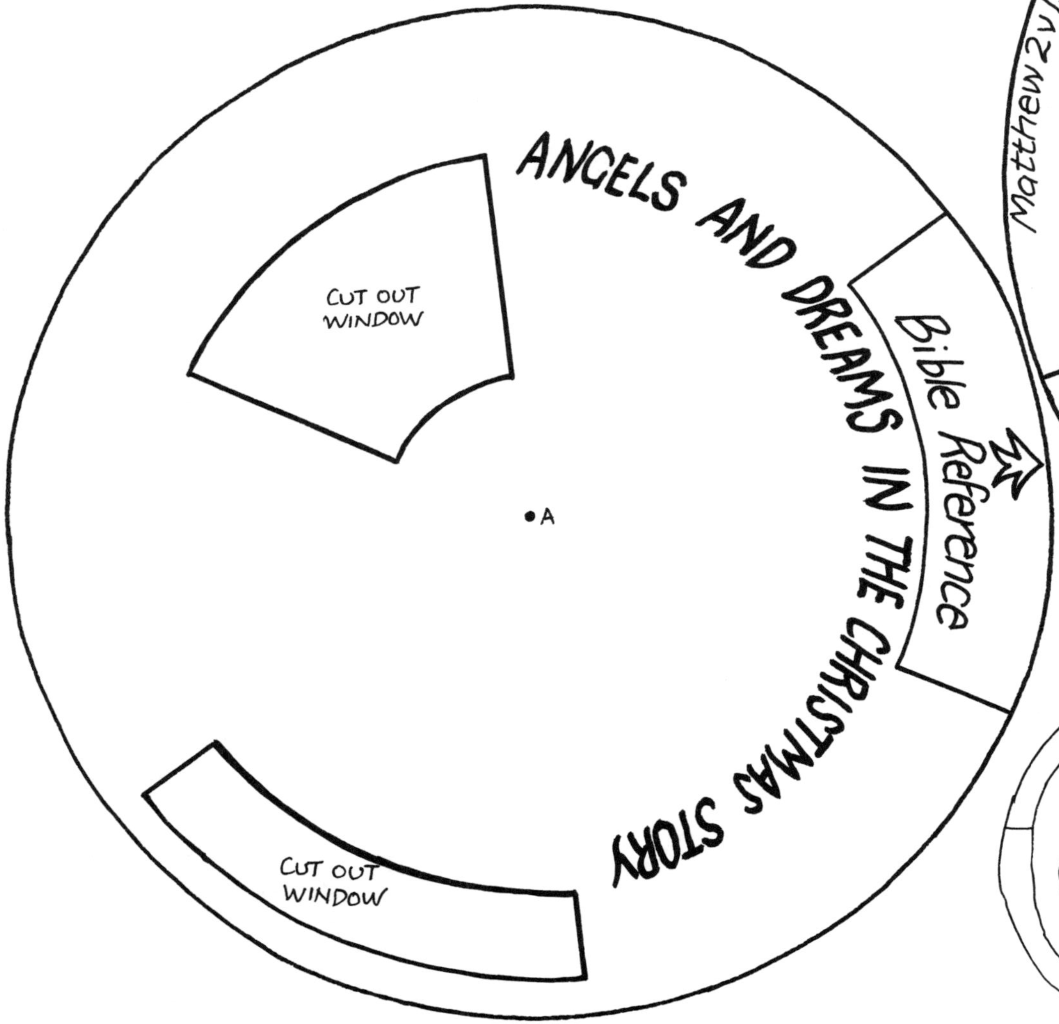

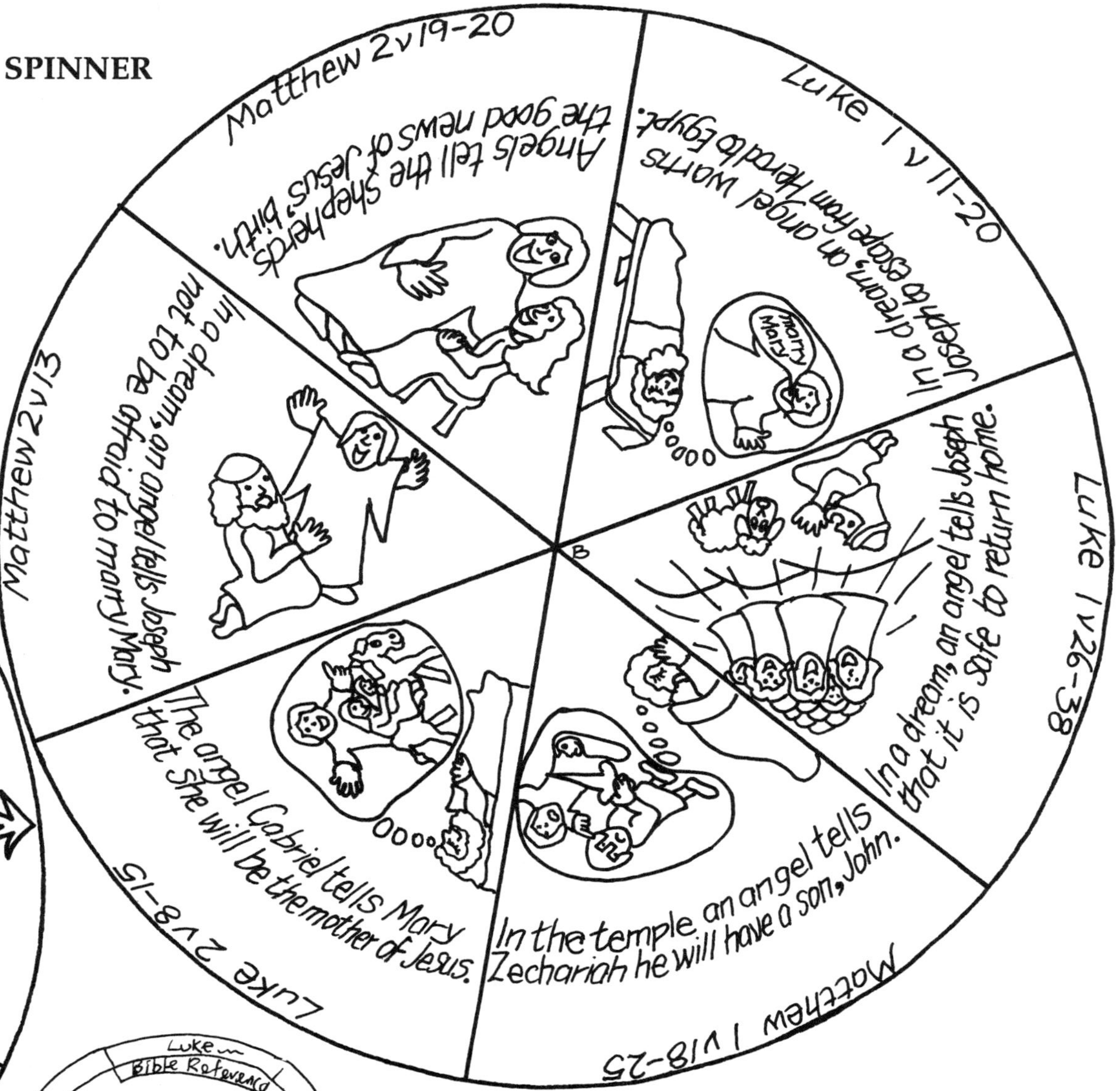

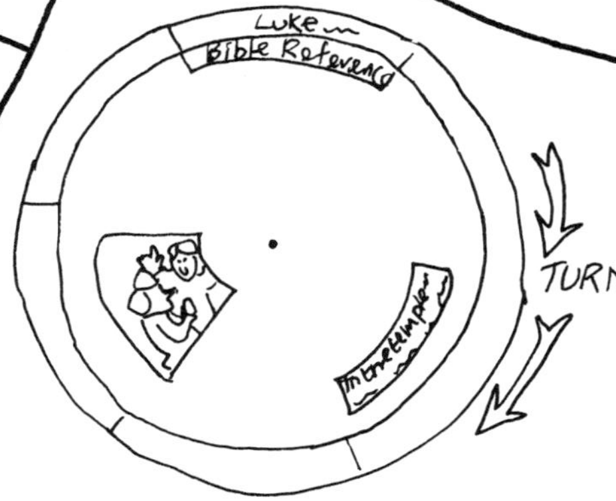

Luke 1 v 26-38 — In a dream an angel tells Joseph that it is safe to return home.

Matthew 1 v 18-25 — In the temple, an angel tells Zechariah he will have a son, John.

Luke 2 v 8-15 — The angel Gabriel tells Mary that she will be the mother of Jesus.

Matthew 2 v 13 — In a dream, an angel tells Joseph not to be afraid to marry Mary.

Matthew 2 v 19-20 — Angels tell the shepherds the good news of Jesus' birth.

Luke 1 v 11-20 — In a dream an angel warns Joseph to escape from Herod to Egypt.

TURN

Luke — Bible Reference

ANGELS AND DREAMS IN THE CHRISTMAS STORY

Bible Reference

• A

CUT OUT WINDOW

CUT OUT WINDOW

31. POP-UP STABLE CHRISTMAS CARD – FIGURES AND ROOF

1. Photocopy this page and following one (32) onto thin card.
2. Cut round outside edge of base.
3. Colour and cut out all pieces on this page.
4. Fold base piece in half first along central line, then open flat again.
5. Cut six slits AB, CD, EF, GH, JK and LM on solid black lines.
6. Carefully fold all dotted lines as shown
   - –·–·–· inwards
   - – – – – outwards

   so that 3 rectangles stand out from card base as shown.
7. Fold stable roof tab inwards along dotted line and glue to dotted rectangle on base card.
8. Glue Mary and Joseph to box FH.
9. Stick shepherd and star in position using sticky fixers (for 3-D effect).
10. Cut slit XY round donkey face, then glue behind nose and stick looking round RH pillar.

OPEN TO SEE SCENE POP UP

STAR

DONKEY

MARY AND JOSEPH WITH BABY JESUS

SHEPHERD

STABLE ROOF

FOLD IN

CUT ROUND OUTLINE

STICK STAR
HERE
USING
STICKY
FIXER

V · W
GLUE STABLE ROOF TAB HERE

A   C   J   L

32. POP-UP STABLE CHRISTMAS CARD – BASE

GLUE STABLE ROOF HERE

GLUE STABLE ROOF HERE

E   G

GLUE MARY
AND JOSEPH
WITH BABY
JESUS HERE.

F   H

B   D   K   M

33. WISE MEN FOLLOW THE STAR – ACTION MODEL

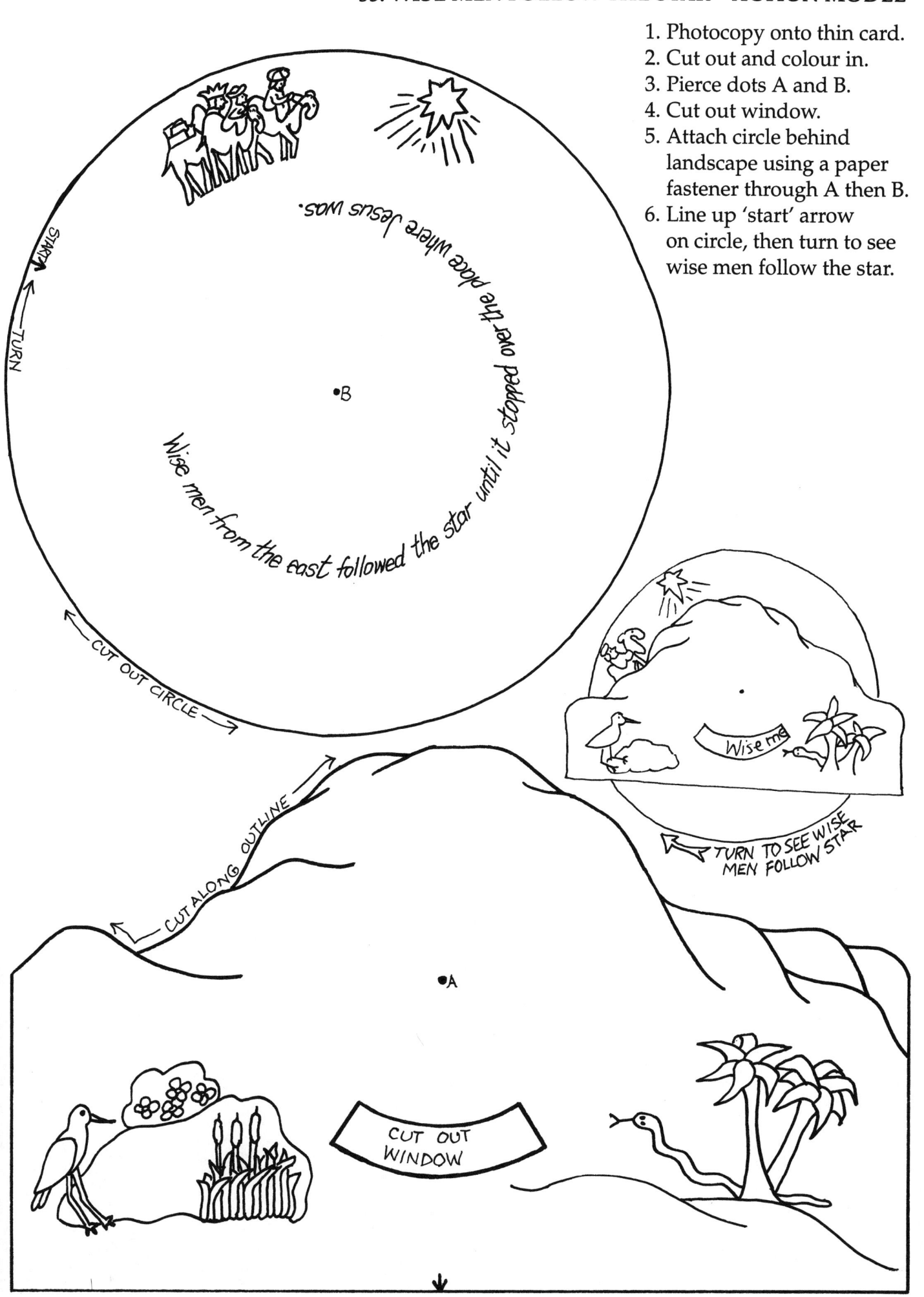

1. Photocopy onto thin card.
2. Cut out and colour in.
3. Pierce dots A and B.
4. Cut out window.
5. Attach circle behind landscape using a paper fastener through A then B.
6. Line up 'start' arrow on circle, then turn to see wise men follow the star.

START
TURN
Wise men from the east followed the star until it stopped over the place where Jesus was.
• B
CUT OUT CIRCLE

CUT ALONG OUTLINE

• A

CUT OUT WINDOW

Wise me

TURN TO SEE WISE MEN FOLLOW STAR

34. SIMEON AND ANNA – ACTION MODEL

1. Photocopy onto thin card.
2. Colour in and cut out, cutting carefully round outline of arm with baby and speech bubble.
3. Cut slits VW and XYZ.
4. Pierce dots A and B.
5. Slot arm with baby up through slit VW from behind picture and speech bubble top through slit XYZ.
6. Join pieces using paper fastener through A then B.

Lord, my eyes have seen your salvation.

PUSH TO SEE SIMEON LIFT BABY JESUS

Read Luke 2 v 22-38

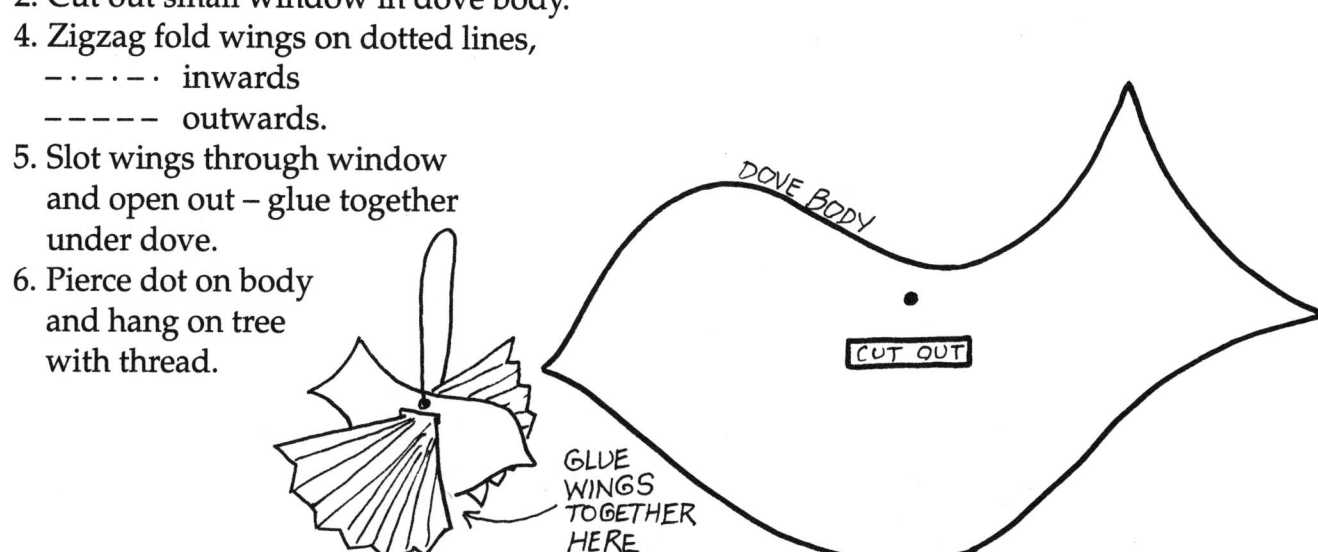

35A. EXPANDING ANGEL DECORATION

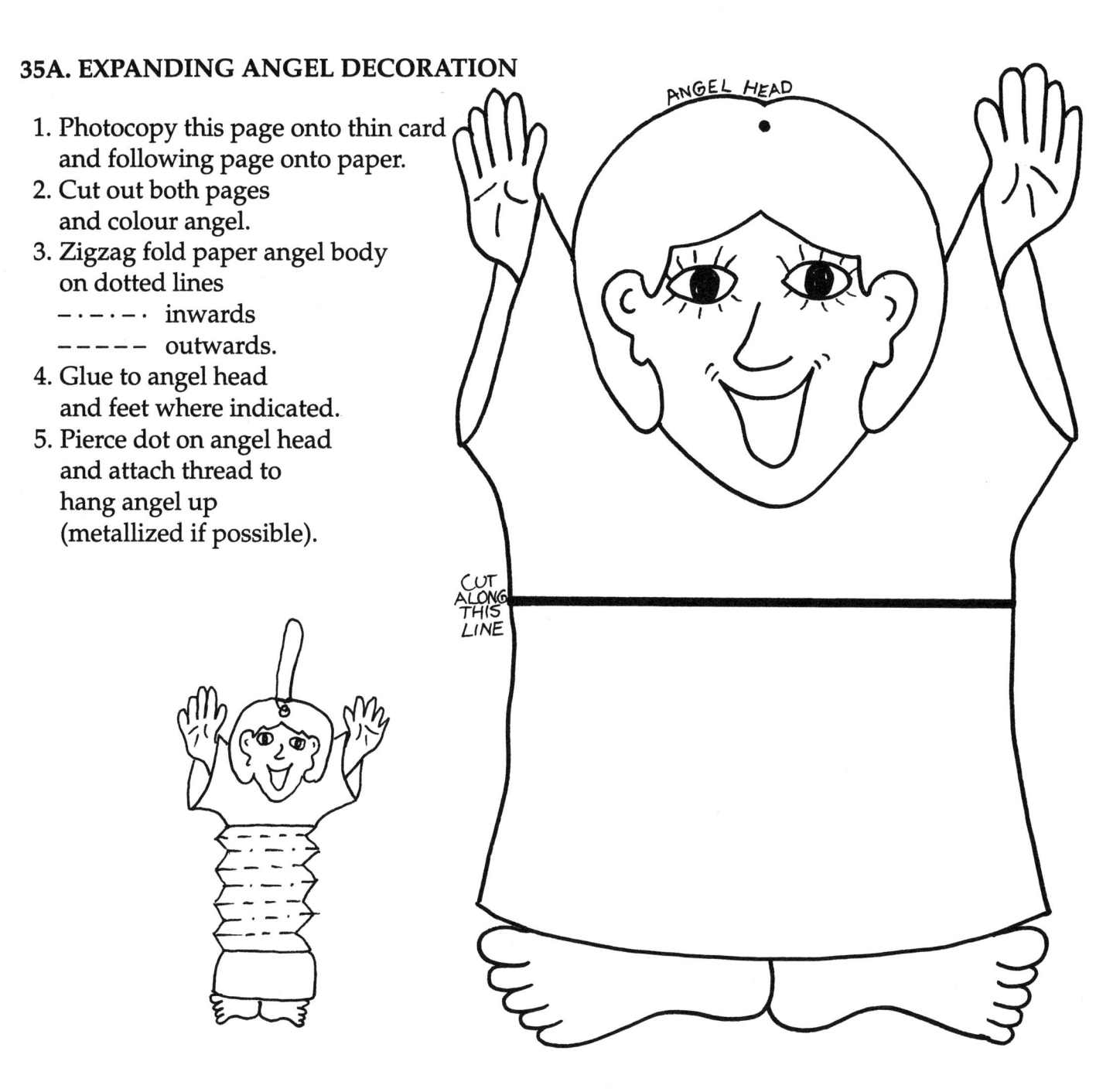

1. Photocopy this page onto thin card and following page onto paper.
2. Cut out both pages and colour angel.
3. Zigzag fold paper angel body on dotted lines
   - – · – · – · inwards
   - – – – – – outwards.
4. Glue to angel head and feet where indicated.
5. Pierce dot on angel head and attach thread to hang angel up (metallized if possible).

ANGEL HEAD

CUT ALONG THIS LINE

35B. DOVE OF PEACE CHRISTMAS TREE DECORATION

1. Photocopy this page onto thin card and following page onto paper.
2. Cut out small window in dove body.
4. Zigzag fold wings on dotted lines,
   - – · – · – · inwards
   - – – – – – outwards.
5. Slot wings through window and open out – glue together under dove.
6. Pierce dot on body and hang on tree with thread.

DOVE BODY

CUT OUT

GLUE WINGS TOGETHER HERE

36A. EXPANDING ANGEL DECORATION – BODY

Photocopy onto **paper**, zig-zag fold and use as instructions on previous page.

ANGEL BODY

GLUE TO ANGEL HEAD

"Do not be afraid.

I bring you good

news of great joy

that will be for

all the people.

Today in the town

of David a Saviour

has been born

to you; he is

Christ the Lord."

GLUE TO ANGEL FEET

36B. DOVE OF PEACE CHRISTMAS TREE DECORATION – WINGS

Photocopy onto paper.

DOVE WINGS

37. CHRISTMAS MOBILE – STABLE ROOF

1. Photocopy this page and following two pages onto thin card.
2. Colour in and cut out all pieces.
3. Glue front and back together for all pieces except star and pierce dots at top for hanging.
4. For star, fold all three pieces inwards on dotted lines and glue all three together to form three-dimensional star. Pierce dots at top and points.
5. Pierce all dots on stable roof, then glue on tab as marked to form roof shape.
6. Attach thread to top of star for hanging up – attach points X, Y, Z to pairs of holes X, Y, Z on stable roof to hang approx. 12cm from roof.
7. Hang figures by threads from appropriate dot i.e. Mary from A etc. Use **hanging** lengths of thread as indicated beside figures – allow extra for tying.

CUT OUT CIRCLE

GLUE ROOF TOGETHER HERE

38. CHRISTMAS MOBILE – STAR, BABY JESUS, ANIMALS

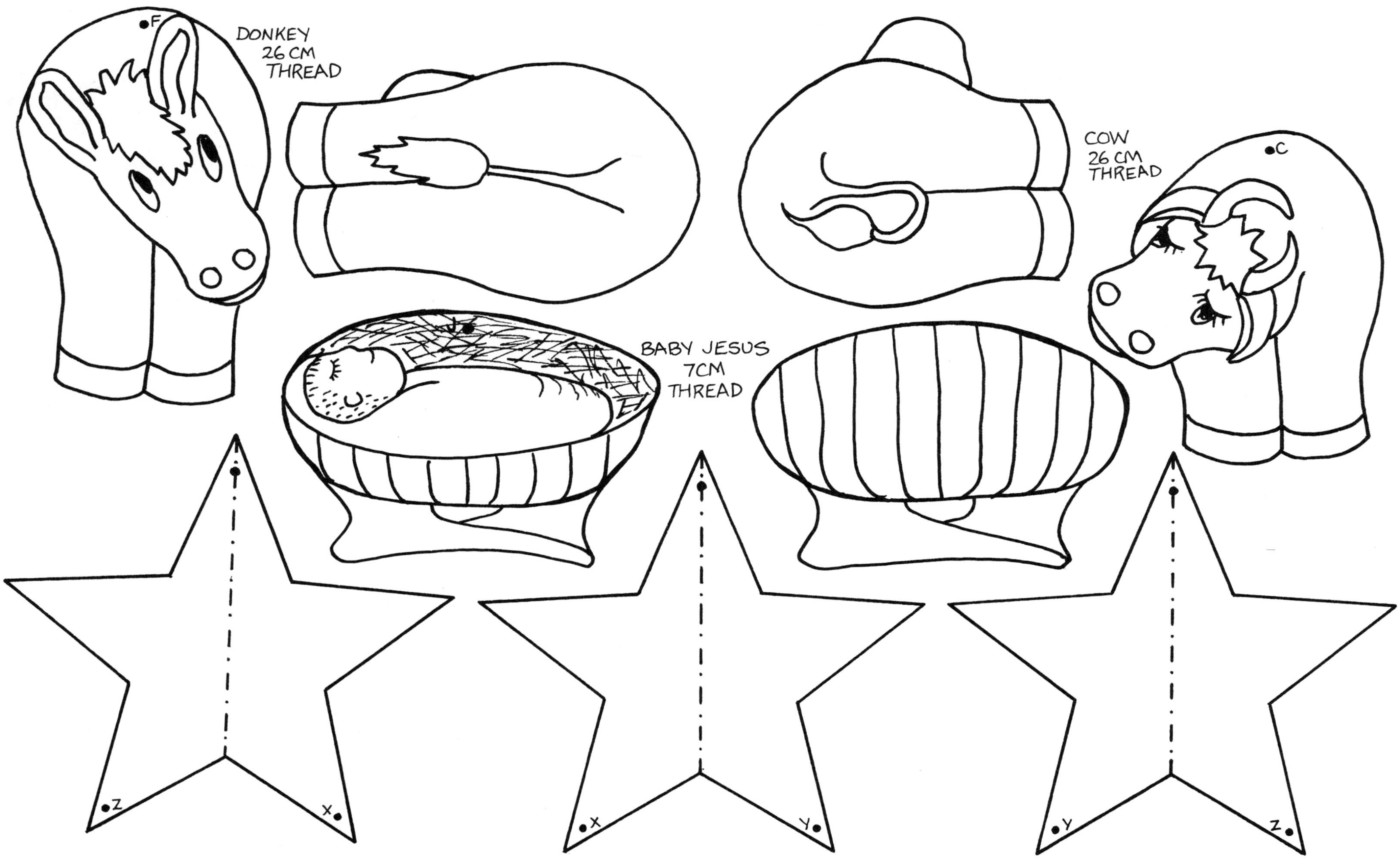

COW
26 CM
THREAD

BABY JESUS
7 CM
THREAD

DONKEY
26 CM
THREAD

39. CHRISTMAS MOBILE – MARY, JOSEPH, KING, SHEPHERD

MARY 7CM THREAD

JOSEPH 7CM THREAD

KING 17CM THREAD

SHEPHERD 17CM THREAD

40. SHEEP FACE BASEBALL CAP

1. Enlarge A4 to A3 size – most photocopiers have a setting for this.
2. Photocopy onto paper or, better still, thin card if you can obtain this in A3 card.
3. Cut slits on parallel lines on top of cap.
4. Cut out cap and ears – colour ears black and staple onto marked spots.
5. Staple AB to CD at back, overlapping to give a good fit.
6. You could use the sheep caps to act out a Christmas play with sheep in it.

41. CHRISTMAS WINDOW PICTURE

1. Photocopy onto TRACING PAPER – use good quality tracing paper, obtainable from art/stationers shops, in A4 size – this should be hand fed through the photocopier.
2. Colour using felt-tip pens for translucent effect.
3. Stick to a window using sticky putty.

ACROSS

1. God's way of warning the wise men (5)
3. The angel brought the shepherds good news of this for all people (5,3)
5. Not a very smart crib (6)
8. Watched by shepherds at night (6)
10. Saw an angel while burning incense in the temple (9)
12. Wanted to kill baby Jesus (5)
14. Jesus means this (7)
16. Jesus' birthplace (9)
18. Caesar Augustus decreed it should be taken (6)
19. He prophesied that a virgin would give birth to a son called Immanuel (6)
21. Widow of eighty-four who never left the temple (4)
22. Place to escape from Herod (5)
24. Number 21 was definitely very this (3)
25. Wise men came from here (4)
27. Joseph belonged to the house and line of this king (5)
28. Angels said, 'Glory to God in the . . . . ' (7)

DOWN

2. A sweet-smelling gift (5)
4. Boys under this age were not safe in Bethlehem (3)
5. He prophesied where Jesus would be born (5)
6. Mary and Joseph travelled from here to Bethlehem (8)
7. Gabriel announced Jesus' birth to her (4)
8. A gift from far away (12)
9. Told by the Holy Spirit he would not die until he had seen the Christ (6)
11. Followed to the baby by foreign visitors (4)
13. He announced the birth of John to Zechariah (7)
14. First visitors to the baby Jesus (9)
15. For not believing, Zechariah was this until his son was born (4)
17. Mother of John (9)
20. Simeon told Mary that this would pierce her own soul (5)
23. A kingly gift (4)
26. The number of months that John was older than Jesus (3)

(If you need help finding the answers have a look in Matthew Chapters 1 and 2, and Luke Chapters 1 and 2.)

43. CHRISTMAS PUZZLE PAGE

Help Mary and Joseph to escape to Egypt through the maze

DECODE THIS VERSE to find out something the angel Gabriel told Mary about Jesus. Move each letter one place forward in the alphabet: a=b, b=c, c=d, z=a, etc.

gd vhkk qdhfm nudq sgd gntrd ne izbna

__ ____ _____ ____ ___ _____ __ _____

enq dudq ghr jhmfcnl vhkk mdudq dmc

___ ____ ___ _____ ____ _____ ___

STABLE JIGSAW – Match the pieces to those on the stable. Write on the words to find out what the angels told the shepherds.

Pieces: Saviour, town, the, Today, Christ, of, he, has, a, David, Lord, in, born;, is, the, been

WORDSEARCH – See how many names of people and places in the Christmas story you can find – there are 14 altogether. (forwards, backwards, up, down, diagonally.)

A	N	N	A	Z	M	A	R	N	A
Z	E	C	A	J	E	G	Y	P	T
M	E	S	E	Z	L	E	J	E	H
E	S	C	L	R	A	J	O	O	D
H	U	X	H	R	S	R	S	J	O
E	S	N	J	A	U	M	E	S	R
L	E	O	H	E	R	O	P	T	E
H	J	E	Y	O	E	I	H	L	H
T	E	M	A	R	J	M	A	R	Y
E	L	I	Z	A	B	E	T	H	O
B	H	S	L	E	I	R	B	A	G

4. ADVENT CALENDAR – PART ONE: FRONT
1. Photocopy this **and following** page onto thin card.
2. NB **before** session with children, adult must cut the doors with craft knife: cut round 3 sides (or curve) on solid lines only – do not fold back at this stage. (Instructions continue on page 45.)

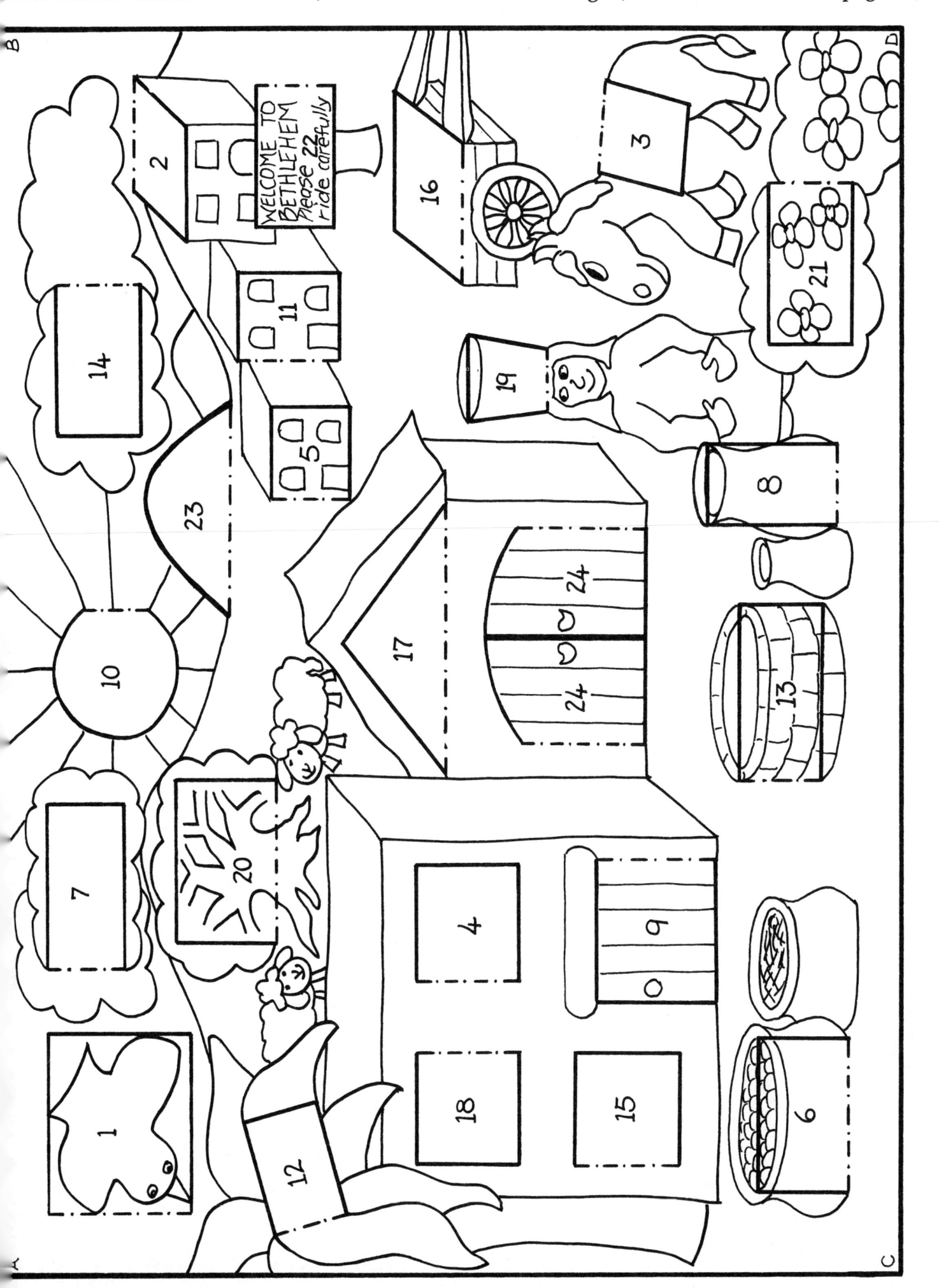

45. ADVENT CALENDAR – PART TWO: BACK
Instructions continued: 3. Cut round outer edge front and back. 4. Colour in both pieces.

5. Glue thin strip round edge of back as marked – place front on top, lining up edges **carefully**, with corners A, B, C, D over A, B, C, D on back.

46. FLIGHT INTO EGYPT – ACTION MODEL

1. Photocopy onto thin card.
2. Colour round outer edge and colour in.
3. Cut off strip along line XY.
4. Cut two curved slits PQ and RS.
5. Pierce dots A and B.
6. Take strip XY – slot X end into slit PQ and Y end into slit RS, so Mary, Joseph and Jesus show on picture.
7. Attach B behind A using paper fastener.
8. Start with Mary and Joseph at QS end – pull X to make Mary and Joseph escape to Egypt with Baby Jesus.

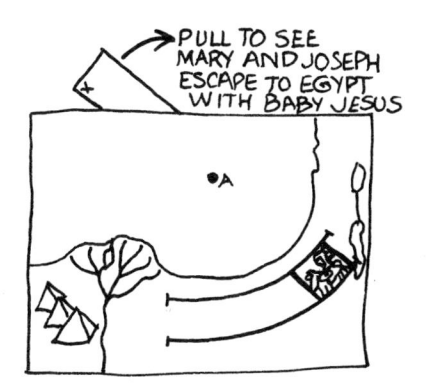

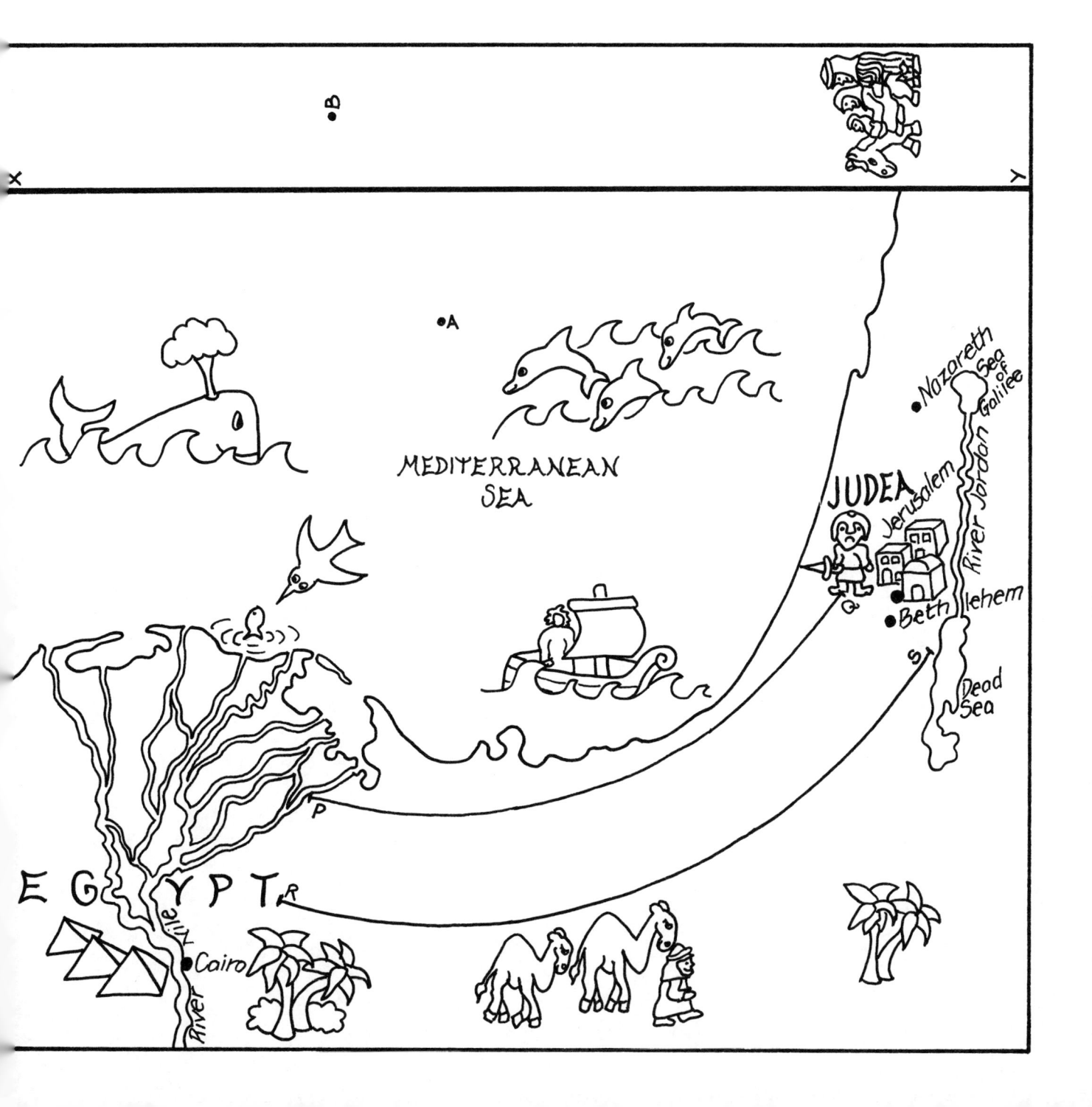